THE OTHER AI

The Art of Instruction

NATURAL CODELEX™

M E TELLEZ

NEURO-IS

ISBN: 979-8-950938-00-9 (Paperback)

The Natural CodeLex™ framework, including the typed instruction layer architecture and deterministic pre-processing method described in this book, is the subject of pending US Patent Application No. 64/090,099, filed June 13, 2026.

Published by NEURO-IS
First Edition, 2026
Printed in the United States of America

THE OTHER AI

The Art of Instruction

Natural CodeLex™

A Systems-Level Framework for AI-Mediated Cognition, Workflow Architecture, and Cognitive Infrastructure

For Barbie, Karina, and Kayla.

My inspiration.
My guardian angel.
My everything.

CHAPTER 1

THE LANGUAGE OF SYSTEMS

Why Prompting Is Cognitive Architecture

Two Users. One System. Opposite Results.

Picture two professionals sitting at identical computers, both opening the same AI system on the same morning. Same model. Same interface. Same underlying technology.

The first types: Write a market analysis for our new product launch.

The system returns four paragraphs. Broad. Vague. Inoffensive. The kind of text that could apply to any product in any industry in any decade. It mentions competitive landscape, customer needs, pricing strategy, and go-to-market timing — all at the same shallow depth, none with specificity. The user reads it, feels mildly disappointed, and wonders whether AI is really as useful as people claim.

The second professional spends ninety seconds constructing something different before sending a single word of substantive instruction:

```
IDENTITY: Senior market strategist specializing
in B2B SaaS competitive positioning.

OBJECTIVE: Analyze competitive positioning for a
workflow automation tool entering mid-market
legal operations.

TARGET SEGMENT: Decision-makers at 50–200 person
law firms.

CONSTRAINTS:
- Focus on switching costs and integration risk
- Ignore consumer legal tech entirely
- Prioritize operational pain points over feature
comparisons
- Do not reference products without documented
market presence
```

```
OUTPUT: Three ranked competitive threats with
supporting rationale and one operational
vulnerability per threat.
```

The system returns a dense, operationally specific analysis. Competitive risks ranked by threat severity. Switching costs examined through the lens of existing case management software dependencies. Integration risk mapped to the specific workflow patterns of small litigation practices. Decision-ready.

Same model. Same intelligence. Same underlying technology. Radically different outputs.

The difference was not cleverness, a secret phrase, or hidden syntax. The difference was architectural. One professional built a cognitive environment. The other asked a question and hoped for the best.

That distinction — between asking a question and architecting an environment — is the foundation of everything in this book. It is the difference between using AI and operating it. Between getting outputs and designing workflows. Between a tool that occasionally surprises you and a system you understand well enough to rely on.

Natural CodeLex exists to close that gap. Not through magic phrases or template libraries, but through a genuine understanding of how probabilistic language systems work, how they fail, how they can be shaped, and how that shaping becomes the basis for serious, high-leverage cognitive work.

1.1 The Misunderstanding at the Heart of AI Culture

Popular AI culture has developed a persistent and operationally destructive mythology around prompting.

The mythology goes like this: somewhere there exists a perfect prompt — a specific combination of words, a particular syntactic structure, a precise sequence of instructions — that reliably unlocks ideal AI output. Find the right phrase and the model performs brilliantly. Use the wrong phrasing and it disappoints. The user's job is to discover the magic words.

This model is not merely incomplete. It actively misleads the people who hold it, pushing them toward behavior that consistently produces worse outcomes than the alternative.

Large language models are not command-line interpreters. They do not parse instructions the way a compiler processes code — deterministically, syntactically, with precise outputs guaranteed by precise inputs. They are probabilistic inference engines. Systems that generate statistically plausible continuations based on patterns learned across enormous bodies of human-generated text, weighted by the specific contextual environment the current prompt creates.

What this means in practice is that prompting is not about control. It is about directional influence. Strong prompts do not force perfect behavior — they reduce ambiguity, improve alignment, and narrow the interpretive spread across which the model must guess. Weak prompts expand that spread, leaving the model to fill uncertainty with statistical averages that feel generic precisely because they are generic.

Norbert Wiener, who founded the field of cybernetics in the 1940s, described control systems not as mechanisms of absolute command but as architectures of feedback and correction operating within probabilistic environments. A thermostat does not force a room to be warm — it creates conditions that make warmth statistically likely through continuous feedback loops. A ship's autopilot does not guarantee a course — it continuously corrects against deviation. Control, in Wiener's framework, was always probabilistic management, never absolute command.

Advanced prompting works identically. The operator does not command the model. The operator shapes the environment in which the model operates — and through that shaping, makes useful outputs more likely while making unhelpful ones less so.

Natural CodeLex begins from this premise: AI outputs are heavily influenced by the structure of the environment surrounding the request. The wording matters. The architecture matters more.

1.2 Language as Architecture

Human beings naturally think of language as communication — a medium for transmitting meaning from one mind to another. Inside AI systems, language serves a second and operationally critical function: it functions as architecture.

The prompt does not merely communicate intent to the model. It constructs the cognitive environment in which the model operates. It shapes what receives attention, what becomes prioritized, what constraints dominate, which concepts become active, and which continuations become statistically likely. Every word is not just a word — it is an architectural decision that affects the probability distribution of everything that follows.

Consider what happens when a model receives a vague instruction: Explain cybersecurity risks.

The model must simultaneously infer the industry context (enterprise? consumer? government?), the organizational scale (startup? Fortune 500?), the intended audience (technical? executive?), the analytical depth required (introductory? expert?), and the most relevant threat categories from hundreds of possibilities. In the absence of architectural constraint, the model defaults to statistical averaging — producing the response most common across all similar requests it has encountered. That response is almost always generic because the average across all contexts is, by definition, specific to none of them.

Now compare that instruction with a structured alternative:

```
OBJECTIVE: Identify operational cybersecurity
risks affecting mid-sized financial institutions.

AUDIENCE: Chief Risk Officer and compliance
leadership.

CONSTRAINTS:
```

```
- Focus on internal process failures, not
external attack vectors
- Ignore consumer phishing — focus on
institutional vulnerabilities
- Prioritize regulatory exposure and audit
failure risk
- Exclude theoretical risks without documented
incident patterns

OUTPUT FORMAT: Ranked risk matrix, 5 items
maximum, severity and likelihood per item.
```

The model itself has not become more intelligent. The environment became more organized. The instruction architecture creates narrower interpretation, clearer prioritization, more stable analytical direction, and an output format that the model can target precisely. The result is not just better — it is specifically useful rather than generically informative.

This is cognitive systems design: using language not merely to communicate intent, but to architect the interpretive environment in which generation occurs. Systems engineering has understood this principle for decades. Well-designed systems do not rely on perfect execution at every step — they rely on structural constraints that make failure less likely and recovery more predictable. Prompting at the advanced level works the same way.

1.3 The Probabilistic Nature of AI Systems

To work effectively with AI systems, operators must genuinely internalize — not just intellectually acknowledge — what probabilistic generation actually means.

Traditional software executes deterministically. Given the same input under the same conditions, a well-written program produces the same output every time. This predictability is the foundation of software reliability. It is also why programmers develop strong intuitions about causation — they can trace from input to output through a chain of logical operations.

Language models do not work this way. The same prompt, sent twice to the same model, can produce meaningfully different outputs — not because the model is broken or inconsistent, but because generation involves sampling from a probability distribution, not executing a deterministic function. The model produces the most plausible continuation given the context, but plausibility is a distribution, not a point.

This has several important operational consequences.

First, evaluation requires multiple samples. A single output is not a reliable indicator of what the model can produce for a given prompt. An output that seems weak may be an unlucky sample from a good distribution. An output that seems strong may be a lucky sample from a poor one. Serious operators test prompts across multiple generations before drawing conclusions about prompt quality.

Second, consistency is a product of design, not a default. Probabilistic systems are variable by nature. Reducing that variability requires explicit architectural choices — tighter constraints, more specific output specifications, identity framing that narrows the behavioral distribution. The operator who complains that AI outputs are inconsistent is often the operator who has done nothing to constrain that inconsistency.

Third, improvement is continuous, not binary. Because outputs sample from distributions, the operator's goal is not to find the prompt that produces a perfect output — it is to design the prompt architecture that shifts the distribution toward useful outputs and away from useless ones. Small architectural improvements compound significantly over many generations.

1.4 The Difference Between Search and Synthesis

Before language models became mainstream, the dominant model of AI assistance was retrieval. You queried a system. The system returned documents, links, or records. You synthesized those results yourself — reading, comparing, evaluating, and drawing conclusions manually.

Language models do something structurally different. They synthesize. Rather than locating information that already exists in a retrievable form, the model generates probabilistic continuations based on patterns, relationships, and contextual inference drawn from training data. The output is not retrieved — it is constructed.

This distinction changes what good AI interaction looks like. In a retrieval system, the user's job is to formulate the right query — to express what they are looking for in terms the indexing system can match. The quality of the query is measured by recall: did it find the relevant documents?

In a synthesis system, the user's job is to architect the right context — to create an environment that makes the synthesis coherent, relevant, and operationally useful. The quality of the context is measured by alignment: does the output address the actual need with appropriate depth and specificity?

Many users still interact with language models as though they were retrieval systems — typing queries and expecting results. This mental model produces consistently disappointing outputs, not because the model is weak, but because the interaction architecture is wrong. The model is not a search engine waiting to be queried. It is a synthesis engine waiting to be directed.

Directing a synthesis engine is an architectural act. It requires thinking not just about what you want to know, but about the interpretive environment that will make the synthesis coherent, the constraints that will keep it focused, and the output specification that will make the result usable.

1.5 Machine Grammar: The Core Framework

Natural CodeLex introduces a structured prompting methodology called Machine Grammar.

Machine Grammar is not a programming language. It is not a secret syntax or a proprietary formula. It is a disciplined approach to context architecture — a set of structural principles designed to reduce ambiguity, improve interpretive clarity, constrain behavioral drift, and stabilize outputs across the inherent variability of probabilistic systems.

The name is deliberate. Grammar, in its linguistic sense, is the rule system that makes communication precise and interpretable — that distinguishes a clear sentence from an ambiguous one, that creates shared meaning between speaker and listener. Machine Grammar applies the same concept to the communication between operator and AI system: a rule system for creating precise, interpretable prompts that reduce the inferential burden on the model and improve the reliability of what it generates.

Machine Grammar emphasizes five structural elements that, when aligned, produce substantially more reliable outputs than unstructured prompting:

```
1. EXPLICIT OBJECTIVES
What must the output accomplish? Not what subject
it should cover, but what operational goal it
must serve. 'Explain cybersecurity risks' is a
subject. 'Identify the three operational
vulnerabilities most likely to trigger regulatory
action in a financial services audit' is an
objective.

2. OPERATIONAL CONSTRAINTS
What should be excluded, prioritized, or bounded?
Constraints are not limitations on the model's
capability — they are precision instruments that
narrow the interpretive field toward the actual
target. Negative constraints (what to exclude)
are as important as positive ones (what to
include).

3. CONTEXTUAL FRAMING
What identity or perspective should dominate the
generation? What organizational context is
relevant? What prior information should the model
treat as established? Framing establishes the
interpretive lens through which the objective
will be pursued.

4. OUTPUT SPECIFICATION
What does a successful result look like
structurally? A ranked list? A narrative
```

```
analysis? A comparison matrix? Specifying the
output format is not merely cosmetic — it gives
the model a target shape to generate toward,
which significantly improves the coherence and
usability of the result.

5. VERIFICATION CRITERIA
How will quality be assessed? What claims need to
be supported? What assumptions should be flagged?
Embedding quality standards into the prompt
architecture itself — rather than evaluating them
after the fact — produces outputs that are
epistemically more reliable.
```

These five elements work together as an integrated architecture, not as independent checkboxes. An objective without constraints produces unfocused output. Constraints without an objective produce arbitrary exclusions. Output specification without framing produces the right shape with the wrong content. The power of Machine Grammar comes from alignment across all five dimensions simultaneously.

Compare these two instructions addressing the same underlying need:

```
WEAK INSTRUCTION:
Help me improve our operations.

MACHINE GRAMMAR STRUCTURE:

IDENTITY: Senior operations consultant with
expertise in B2B SaaS onboarding.

OBJECTIVE: Identify operational inefficiencies
reducing customer retention in the first 90 days
post-purchase.

CONSTRAINTS:
- Focus on onboarding process failures only
- Exclude product features and pricing —
operational process only
- Ignore marketing and sales pipeline issues
- Prioritize failures with direct behavioral
evidence over theoretical risks

OUTPUT:
```

```
- Ranked bottlenecks by retention impact
- Root cause for each bottleneck
- Observable symptom that identifies each failure
in practice

VERIFICATION: Flag any finding that relies on
assumption rather than documented operational
pattern.
```

The second structure does not guarantee perfection. No prompt architecture does — probabilistic systems remain probabilistic. But it substantially narrows the distribution of possible outputs toward the useful range, while the first instruction leaves the model to guess at nearly every dimension of what 'help me improve our operations' might actually mean.

1.6 The Attention Problem

One of the least understood and most practically important properties of language models is attentional competition.

Language models process prompts by distributing attention across the contextual inputs — assigning weights to different elements based on their salience, position, and relationships to other elements. Every instruction inside a prompt competes for this attentional allocation. Every paragraph, every example, every repeated phrase, every irrelevant detail — each consumes a portion of the model's active attentional capacity.

This creates a counterintuitive operational reality: more information does not automatically improve output quality. Beyond a certain density, additional information begins creating attentional friction — competing with high-priority signals for the same allocative capacity, forcing the model to distribute attention across more material while the actual target becomes relatively less prominent.

Claude Shannon's mathematical theory of communication, developed at Bell Labs in the late 1940s, formalized this tension as the signal-to-noise ratio: the proportion of a communication channel's capacity carrying useful information versus interference. Shannon demonstrated that as noise increases relative to signal, the channel's effective information-carrying capacity decreases — not linearly, but in ways that compound quickly as noise approaches channel capacity.

AI context windows operate under an analogous constraint. A prompt crowded with redundant instructions, repeated objectives, emotional qualifiers, and contextually irrelevant material generates attentional noise. The model attempts to process everything simultaneously, and the result is diluted reasoning — outputs that reflect the statistical average across all the competing signals rather than the precise target of the highest-priority ones.

Advanced operators focus heavily on signal density: the ratio between relevant contextual guidance and unnecessary informational noise. The strongest prompts are not necessarily the longest. They are the most coherently structured — where every element earns its presence by meaningfully contributing to the interpretive environment rather than simply filling space.

1.7 Constraint Management

The relationship between constraints and AI capability is one of the most counterintuitive aspects of advanced prompting, and one of the most important to internalize correctly.

Most users assume that constraints limit AI capability — that telling the model what not to do reduces the quality of what it produces. In practice, the opposite is frequently true.

When prompts are unconstrained, the model faces maximum interpretive uncertainty. It must determine not just what to say, but what to prioritize, what tone to use, what level of detail is appropriate, what analytical framework to apply, and what output structure makes sense — all simultaneously, with no guidance. Under this uncertainty, the model defaults to statistical averaging across all similar requests. The output covers the most common ground at the most common depth in the most common format. It is generically correct and specifically useless.

Constraints eliminate guessing. A scope constraint that excludes marketing analysis allows the model to allocate its full analytical capacity to operational analysis. A tone constraint that specifies executive communication frees the model from stylistic uncertainty. A source constraint that limits the model to provided documents eliminates hallucination risk from outside-information assumptions. Each constraint removes a dimension of uncertainty that was previously consuming generative capacity without contributing to the actual goal.

This mirrors the principle that professional disciplines have understood intuitively for centuries. Architecture produces more elegant solutions when working within structural and site constraints than when given unlimited freedom. Poetry's most durable forms — the sonnet, the haiku, the villanelle — achieve extraordinary expression through extreme formal restriction. Engineering produces safer, more elegant designs when specifications are precise rather than open-ended. The constraint is not the enemy of quality. Poorly designed constraints are the enemy of quality. Well-designed constraints are its architecture.

1.8 Iteration Is the Real Workflow

One of the most persistent and damaging misconceptions in AI usage is the expectation that first outputs should be final.

This expectation is understandable. Human beings associate speed and fluency with competence. When a system returns a polished, grammatically correct, professionally structured response in seconds, the psychological pressure to accept it as complete is significant. Questioning it feels like ingratitude, or like an implicit admission that the prompt was inadequate.

Advanced operators have shed this psychological dynamic entirely. They understand that first outputs are provisional — the model's best guess under the maximum interpretive uncertainty that exists before any refinement has occurred.

The first output is calibration data. It reveals the model's default assumptions, its interpretive tendencies, and the gaps between what was specified and what was needed. It is the beginning of a workflow, not the end of one.

Consider a realistic refinement sequence for a strategic analysis task:

```
ROUND 1 – Initial output:
Too broad. Covers all possible strategic
variables without prioritization.
Diagnosis: Objective too vague. Interpretive
field too wide.
Refinement: Narrow to competitive positioning
analysis only. Ignore internal operations.

ROUND 2 – Second output:
Better scope. Now addresses competitive landscape
with some specificity.
Remaining issue: Analysis is descriptive rather
than evaluative. No prioritization.
Refinement: Rank threats by operational impact.
Assign urgency ratings. Remove descriptive
overview – get to findings directly.

ROUND 3 – Third output:
Dense, prioritized, evaluative. Approaching
target quality.
Remaining issue: Confident assertions without
clear evidentiary basis.
Refinement: Adversarial review – challenge each
finding. Identify unsupported assumptions. Flag
low-confidence claims.

ROUND 4 – Final output:
Ranked findings with explicit confidence levels.
Assumptions flagged. Decision-ready.
Outcome: Four iterations producing output that no
single prompt could have generated.
```

Each iteration is not a correction of failure. It is a calibration step — progressively narrowing the model's interpretive field toward the actual target, revealing and correcting misalignments, improving signal density. The process is not an admission that the first prompt was wrong. It is the normal operational behavior of a probabilistic system being directed toward a precise target through successive approximation.

1.9 The Illusion of Intelligence and the Reality of Instability

AI systems feel intelligent partly because fluent language feels intelligent.

When outputs are coherent, articulate, professionally structured, and contextually adaptive, humans naturally infer understanding. This is not a cognitive failure — it is a deeply rational heuristic in a world where, historically, producing fluent, contextually appropriate language required the kind of understanding that language typically signals. The problem is that this heuristic fails systematically when applied to AI systems.

In 1966, MIT researcher Joseph Weizenbaum built ELIZA — a simple pattern-matching program that simulated a psychotherapist by reflecting user statements back as questions. The program had no understanding of language, no model of human psychology, no reasoning capacity of any kind. It matched input patterns to response templates. Despite this, users consistently attributed understanding, empathy, and genuine concern to the system. Some refused to accept that ELIZA was not a real therapist. Weizenbaum was disturbed enough by this response that he spent the rest of his career writing about the dangers of anthropomorphizing computers.

The ELIZA effect has only intensified as AI systems have become more capable. When a model speaks consistently, maintains logical coherence across a long conversation, uses professional vocabulary appropriately, and simulates the structural features of expertise, humans instinctively perceive intelligence and understanding. The perception is not entirely wrong — something sophisticated is happening. But it is not the same kind of understanding that human expertise involves, and the gap between the two matters enormously in high-stakes applications.

Hallucinations — confident, fluent, plausible-sounding outputs that contain factually incorrect or logically invalid claims — are the most visible symptom of this gap. But the instability runs deeper than hallucination. Language models can generate outputs that are factually accurate, grammatically correct, and structurally sophisticated while containing subtle reasoning errors, unsupported inferences, or framing choices that systematically distort the analysis.

Advanced operators maintain disciplined skepticism calibrated to stakes. For low-stakes creative or drafting work, they may accept outputs with minimal verification. For analytical work that informs consequential decisions, they treat AI outputs as drafts requiring expert review, adversarial challenge, and source verification — regardless of how authoritative those outputs appear. The fluency that makes AI outputs feel reliable is precisely the feature that makes uncritical acceptance dangerous.

1.10 The Shift From User to Operator

The most important distinction in AI usage is not between beginners and experts. It is between users and operators.

A user asks: Can the AI help me with this? Their mental model positions the AI as a service — something that either can or cannot perform the requested function. When outputs disappoint, the user concludes that the AI is limited. When outputs succeed, the user attributes the success to the AI's capability. The user's role is to make requests. The system's role is to fulfill them.

An operator asks: How should this workflow be architected? Their mental model positions the AI as a probabilistic system — something whose output quality is heavily determined by the environment in which it operates. When outputs disappoint, the operator examines the contextual architecture and identifies what needs adjustment. When outputs succeed, the operator analyzes what worked and systematizes it. The operator's role is to design the system. The AI's role is to generate within it.

This shift is not primarily a technical skill. It is a mental model shift — a fundamental reorientation in how the relationship between human and AI system is understood. Users become frustrated with AI. Operators become more effective with it over time, because every interaction produces information about what works and what does not, which compounds into increasingly sophisticated workflow architecture.

Natural CodeLex is fundamentally a framework for making the mental model shift from user to operator — from asking questions and hoping for results to designing environments and managing systems.

1.11 Failure Modes

Understanding failure is as important as understanding success in any systems context. Language models have consistent, predictable failure modes that operators can learn to anticipate, recognize, and mitigate.

HALLUCINATION: The generation of plausible, fluent, confident-sounding content that is factually incorrect or logically invalid. Hallucination is not random — it tends to cluster in specific conditions: topics where training data is thin or conflicting, numerical claims, specific citations and references, recent events, and highly technical domains where plausible-sounding language diverges significantly from precise truth.

CONTEXT CONTAMINATION: The blending of incompatible contextual signals across a long or multi-topic session, producing outputs that inappropriately combine styles, analytical frameworks, or constraints from different parts of the conversation. A forensic audit session that drifts into casual conversation will typically see audit precision degrade as conversational patterns contaminate the analytical context.

OVERGENERALIZATION: The default to broad, generic outputs that cover the statistical average across all similar requests rather than the specific need at hand. Overgeneral outputs are the predictable result of underspecified prompts

— they are not model failures but appropriate responses to insufficient architectural guidance.

CONFIDENCE MISCALIBRATION: The generation of outputs with uniform apparent confidence regardless of the actual evidentiary support behind specific claims. Language models do not naturally distinguish between well-supported conclusions and speculative inferences unless explicitly instructed to do so.

CONSTRAINT DECAY: The gradual weakening of constraints established early in a session as new context enters the window and earlier instructions lose attentional salience. A constraint that strongly shapes output in the first three exchanges may have little influence by exchange twenty if it has not been reinforced.

Each failure mode has a corresponding mitigation strategy: source constraints and adversarial review for hallucination, session segmentation for context contamination, tight objective specification for overgeneralization, explicit verification requirements for confidence miscalibration, and periodic reinforcement for constraint decay. The operator who knows the failure modes can design around them proactively rather than encountering them reactively.

Final Principle: Cognitive Infrastructure

Prompting is not ultimately about talking to machines. It is about designing cognitive environments that influence how synthetic systems interpret, prioritize, and generate meaning.

This framing has implications that extend well beyond individual productivity. As AI systems become embedded into business, education, media, and governance, they increasingly function as cognitive infrastructure — systems that shape how large numbers of people access, process, and act on information. Understanding how to interact effectively with probabilistic cognitive systems is not just a professional advantage. It is becoming a form of structural literacy for navigating an AI-mediated world.

The wording matters. The architecture matters more. The iteration matters most. And beneath all three lies the mental model shift that makes everything else possible: the movement from user to operator, from asking questions to designing systems, from hoping for outputs to engineering environments.

That shift is what Natural CodeLex is built to accelerate.

CHAPTER 2

FROM CORPUS TO CORELEX™

The Evolution of Contextual Cognition in AI Systems

Every field that works seriously with language eventually confronts the same foundational question: what is the relationship between the collection of language a system has access to and the quality of reasoning that system can produce?

In linguistics and natural language processing, that question produced the concept of the corpus — the curated collection of text that defines the informational universe within which a system operates. Understanding what a corpus is, how it has been used, and where its conceptual limits lie is not merely historical background. It is the foundation for understanding what Natural CodeLex™ introduces through CoreLex™ — and why that introduction represents a meaningful evolution rather than simply a rebranding of existing ideas.

This chapter traces the intellectual lineage honestly and precisely: from traditional corpus linguistics through modern AI memory architectures, to the CoreLex model that Natural CodeLex proposes as a next-stage framework for synthetic contextual cognition. The goal is not to overclaim — the underlying components of this evolution existed before this framework named them. The goal is to show what becomes possible when those components are synthesized into a unified architecture for persistent cognitive continuity.

2.1 The Traditional Corpus: Origins and Function

The word corpus comes from the Latin for body — and the metaphor is precise. A corpus is a body of text: a structured, principled collection of written or spoken language assembled for the purpose of linguistic analysis, computational processing, or statistical modeling.

Corpus linguistics as a formal discipline emerged in the mid-twentieth century, when researchers began moving away from introspective analysis of language — what grammarians believed language should do — toward empirical analysis of language as it actually appeared in real use. The Brown Corpus, assembled at Brown University in the 1960s, was among the first large-scale computerized text collections: one million words of American English drawn from 500 text samples across 15 categories of written language. It was a radical methodological commitment to evidence over intuition.

The traditional corpus served several distinct functions across its history of use:

```
TRAINING FUNCTION:
Corpora provided the raw material from which
statistical models of language could be
constructed. Early speech recognition systems,
machine translation engines, and spelling
correctors all depended on large text corpora to
build probabilistic models of how words, phrases,
and grammatical structures co-occurred in natural
language.

BENCHMARKING FUNCTION:
Corpora provided standardized evaluation datasets
against which competing systems could be
measured. If two machine translation systems were
both evaluated against the same reference corpus,
their performance could be compared objectively.
The corpus was the shared ground truth.

RETRIEVAL FUNCTION:
As information retrieval systems developed,
corpora became the indexed collections that
search engines queried. A legal research corpus
contained case law. A scientific literature
corpus contained journal articles. The user
queried the corpus; the corpus returned relevant
documents. The corpus was a library; the system
was a librarian.

STATISTICAL MODELING FUNCTION:
N-gram models, hidden Markov models, and early
neural language models all learned the
statistical properties of language from corpora —
```

> the probability that a given word follows a given sequence of words, the likelihood of specific syntactic structures, the distributional patterns that define semantic similarity. The corpus was data; the model was a statistical summary of that data.

What all of these functions share is a fundamental orientation: the corpus is passive. It is a repository. It stores. It supplies. It is queried. The intelligence — such as it was — resided in the models trained on the corpus or the algorithms that retrieved from it. The corpus itself was inert. A collection of text. A body of evidence. A static artifact.

This passivity was not a limitation anyone felt acutely, because the systems using corpora were themselves relatively limited. Early NLP systems were rule-based or statistical — they did not engage in open-ended reasoning, did not maintain contextual continuity across extended interactions, and did not generate language in the flexible, generative way that large language models do. The corpus as static repository was adequate for the systems it served.

The arrival of large language models changed what the context environment needed to do — and exposed the inadequacy of the passive corpus model for the new generation of AI interaction.

2.2 The LLM Era: What Changed and What Didn't

Large language models represent a qualitative shift in what AI systems can do with language. They do not merely retrieve from corpora or apply statistical patterns learned from them. They generate — producing novel language that integrates patterns from training in ways that resemble reasoning, analysis, and synthesis rather than simple retrieval or pattern matching.

This generative capability created new possibilities and new problems simultaneously. The new possibilities are evident: LLMs can engage in extended analytical conversation, produce sophisticated synthesized text across domains, reason through complex problems with apparent flexibility, and adapt their outputs to specific contextual requirements in ways that no previous system could match.

The new problems were less immediately visible. LLMs do not have persistent memory between sessions. Their context window — the working cognitive environment for any given interaction — resets completely when a session ends. Every new session begins from the same baseline: the model's training, and nothing more. All the contextual architecture established in a prior session, all the interpretive frameworks constructed through careful prompt design, all the semantic continuity built up through extended collaboration — gone.

The field responded to this limitation by developing several memory and persistence architectures, each addressing a different aspect of the continuity problem:

```
CONTEXT WINDOW EXPANSION:
Increasing the size of the context window allows
more prior conversation to remain active within a
single session. Modern LLMs support context
windows of hundreds of thousands of tokens —
enough to hold entire books within a single
session. This helps with within-session
continuity but does nothing for cross-session
persistence.

RETRIEVAL-AUGMENTED GENERATION (RAG):
RAG systems maintain external knowledge bases —
typically vector databases of document embeddings
— that can be queried dynamically during
generation. When a user asks a question, the
system retrieves relevant document chunks from
the knowledge base and injects them into the
active context window. This allows AI systems to
draw on large, updatable knowledge repositories
without those repositories needing to fit within
a single context window.

VECTOR MEMORY SYSTEMS:
Vector databases store text as high-dimensional
numerical representations (embeddings) that
capture semantic meaning. Similar concepts
cluster near each other in vector space, enabling
semantic search — retrieving not just exact
matches but conceptually related content. Vector
memory systems allow AI agents to maintain large
```

```
knowledge bases and retrieve relevant material
based on conceptual similarity rather than
keyword matching.

PERSISTENT CHAT MEMORY:
Modern AI platforms including Claude, ChatGPT,
and others maintain memory systems that store
facts, preferences, and context from prior
conversations. 'User prefers concise responses.'
'Prior project involved healthcare compliance.'
These memories are injected into future sessions
to provide personalization and basic continuity.

SESSION SUMMARIES AND AGENT MEMORY:
More sophisticated agent architectures maintain
structured summaries of prior work – what was
accomplished, what decisions were made, what
remains outstanding – and inject these summaries
into new sessions to provide operational
continuity across extended projects.
```

Each of these architectures addresses a real limitation. Each represents genuine engineering progress. And each shares a fundamental orientation that, on examination, reveals an important conceptual gap.

Every one of these memory architectures is primarily retrieval-oriented. They store information and retrieve it. Preferences, facts, prior conversation summaries, document chunks — all of these are information artifacts that can be stored and retrieved. What they do not preserve is something more fundamental: the interpretive architecture through which information becomes meaningful.

This is the distinction that Natural CodeLex and CoreLex address.

2.3 The Gap Between Memory and Cognition

To understand what CoreLex introduces, it is essential to understand precisely what current memory architectures do not do.

Consider a realistic scenario. An operator spends three sessions developing a complex strategic analysis framework with an AI system. In those sessions, they have established:

> - A specific analytical identity (senior enterprise risk auditor) with defined evidentiary standards
> - A proprietary terminology system for classifying risk types
> - A reasoning framework that prioritizes regulatory exposure over reputational risk
> - A set of contextual assumptions about the organization's specific situation
> - A semantic architecture that defines relationships between twelve different risk categories
> - An ongoing analytical thread connecting findings from sessions one and two

When session four begins, current memory systems might restore: 'User is working on risk analysis for a financial services firm. Prior sessions established twelve risk categories.' That is information retrieval. It tells the model what the prior work was about.

What it does not restore is the cognitive architecture — the active interpretive framework that governed how the model reasoned about risk, what it prioritized, how it weighted competing considerations, what semantic relationships it maintained between concepts, and what analytical momentum the work had developed. The operator must reconstruct this architecture manually, re-establishing constraints, re-framing identity, re-building the interpretive environment from scratch.

The difference is between remembering that you were doing a puzzle and remembering exactly where you were in solving it — which pieces are placed, what patterns you were pursuing, what hypotheses you were testing. Memory systems restore the former. CoreLex is a framework for preserving the latter.

This distinction maps onto a well-established distinction in cognitive science between declarative memory (memory of facts and events — what you know) and procedural memory (memory of how to do things — how you reason). Current AI memory architectures are almost entirely declarative. They remember facts about prior work. CoreLex addresses what might be called interpretive continuity — the preservation of the reasoning architecture and cognitive posture through which those facts become meaningful.

2.4 Natural CodeLex and the CoreLex Model

CoreLex is the foundational conceptual architecture of Natural CodeLex. It represents the framework's answer to a question that existing corpus and memory architectures have not fully addressed: how do you maintain not just informational continuity but cognitive continuity across extended AI-mediated workflows?

The definition that Natural CodeLex proposes:

```
CoreLex – The foundational contextual language
substrate through which AI systems maintain
interpretive continuity, semantic weighting,
attention allocation, and probabilistic reasoning
behavior across extended AI-mediated workflows.

Unlike traditional corpora, which function as
passive information repositories, and unlike
standard memory systems, which function as
retrieval-oriented persistence architectures,
CoreLex is an active contextual cognition
environment – a deliberately constructed
operating layer that shapes how a system reasons
rather than merely what it knows.
```

This definition requires unpacking, because each element carries operational weight.

CONTEXTUAL LANGUAGE SUBSTRATE: CoreLex is not a document or a database. It is a substrate — a foundational layer on which cognitive activity occurs. In materials science, a substrate is the material on which something else is deposited or grown. The substrate's properties fundamentally shape what can be built on it. CoreLex functions analogously: the properties of the contextual substrate — its terminology, its analytical frameworks, its identity architecture, its constraint structure — fundamentally shape the cognitive activity that occurs within it.

INTERPRETIVE CONTINUITY: The emphasis is on continuity of interpretation, not continuity of information. Two sessions operating within the same CoreLex substrate will interpret new information through the same analytical lens, apply the same evidentiary standards, maintain the same terminological consistency, and pursue the same reasoning trajectories. This is qualitatively different from two sessions that happen to have access to the same stored facts.

SEMANTIC WEIGHTING: Within a CoreLex environment, concepts do not carry uniform weight. The substrate establishes a hierarchy of salience — which concepts are central, which are peripheral, which relationships between concepts are structurally important. This weighting shapes attention allocation throughout the session, ensuring that the model's generative capacity is concentrated on the dimensions that matter most within the specific analytical context.

PROBABILISTIC REASONING BEHAVIOR: Ultimately, CoreLex functions by shifting the probability distributions that govern generation — making certain analytical directions more likely, certain conclusions more accessible, certain reasoning patterns more dominant. It does not force outputs. It shapes the probability landscape within which generation occurs.

2.5 The Architecture of a CoreLex Environment

A CoreLex environment is not a single document or instruction block. It is a layered architecture constructed from multiple components that together create a stable, persistent cognitive operating environment.

```
COMPONENT 1 — TERMINOLOGICAL ARCHITECTURE:
The CoreLex environment establishes precise,
stable terminology for the domain of work. Terms
are defined explicitly and consistently — not
assumed from general usage. When a CoreLex
environment defines 'operational risk' as meaning
specifically 'failures in internal processes that
create regulatory exposure,' that definition
governs all analysis within the environment.
```

Terminological consistency prevents the semantic drift that degrades analytical quality across extended work.

COMPONENT 2 — IDENTITY AND ANALYTICAL POSTURE:
The CoreLex environment specifies the professional identity and analytical philosophy that governs reasoning. Not just 'act as an auditor' but a fully specified analytical posture: what evidentiary standards apply, what risk orientation dominates, what communication style governs output, what priorities are structurally embedded in the reasoning architecture.

COMPONENT 3 — CONCEPTUAL FRAMEWORK ARCHITECTURE:
The CoreLex environment maps the conceptual territory of the domain — the relationships between key concepts, the analytical frameworks through which problems will be approached, the classification systems that will organize findings. This framework architecture ensures that each session builds within the same conceptual structure rather than constructing a new one from scratch.

COMPONENT 4 — CONSTRAINT INHERITANCE:
The CoreLex environment carries forward the operational constraints established in prior work — what to exclude, what to prioritize, what sources to trust, what standards to apply. These constraints persist across sessions not as retrieved preferences but as embedded architectural properties of the cognitive environment.

COMPONENT 5 — REASONING MOMENTUM:
Perhaps most distinctively, the CoreLex environment preserves the analytical trajectory established in prior work — what hypotheses are active, what threads remain unresolved, what the next analytical steps are, where the current analysis sits within the larger project. This is the cognitive equivalent of preserving not just your notes but your train of thought.

Together, these five components create something qualitatively different from either a document corpus or a memory system. They create an active cognitive operating environment — a persistent interpretive context within which each new session begins not from a blank slate, but from the accumulated analytical architecture of all prior work.

2.6 How CoreLex Differs From What Came Before

The intellectual honesty this framework requires means stating clearly what CoreLex is not, as much as what it is.

> CORELEX™ IS NOT A CORPUS IN THE TRADITIONAL SENSE:
> A traditional corpus is a collection of text used as training data, retrieval source, or benchmarking material. CoreLex is not a text collection. It is a cognitive architecture specification – a structured description of how a system should reason, not what information it should draw on. A corpus answers 'what does the system know?' CoreLex answers 'how does the system think?'
>
> CORELEX™ IS NOT RAG:
> Retrieval-augmented generation enhances AI outputs by retrieving relevant document chunks from external knowledge bases. RAG is information-oriented – it brings relevant facts into the active context. CoreLex is cognition-oriented – it establishes the interpretive framework within which those facts become meaningful. RAG without CoreLex retrieves relevant information but may interpret it inconsistently across sessions. CoreLex without RAG maintains consistent interpretation but may lack comprehensive factual grounding. The two are complementary, not competing.
>
> CORELEX™ IS NOT PERSISTENT CHAT MEMORY:
> Persistent chat memory stores facts and preferences from prior conversations and injects them into future sessions. 'User is working on a legal compliance project.' This is retrieval-oriented persistence. CoreLex maintains the reasoning architecture – the analytical identity, the constraint structure, the conceptual framework, the interpretive posture – that determines how the system engages with that project. The difference is between knowing you

```
were working on something and knowing how you
were thinking about it.

CORELEX™ IS NOT AN AGENT ARCHITECTURE:
Agent systems use memory to enable multi-step
autonomous task execution. They remember what
steps have been completed and what remains.
CoreLex is not about task completion tracking –
it is about cognitive continuity. It preserves
not just what has been done but how the system
has been thinking, enabling a form of
intellectual continuity that task-tracking
architectures do not address.
```

What CoreLex adds, relative to all of these existing architectures, is the explicit recognition that the quality of AI-mediated cognitive work depends not just on what information is available but on the stability and coherence of the interpretive framework through which that information is processed. And that this interpretive framework can be deliberately constructed, persistently maintained, and transferred across sessions in ways that preserve cognitive continuity far more completely than information retrieval alone.

2.7 Building a CoreLex Environment: Practical Architecture

The theoretical distinction between CoreLex and prior architectures becomes operational through specific practices. The following demonstrates what a CoreLex environment actually looks like in construction and deployment.

A CoreLex environment is typically instantiated through a structured initialization block — a dense, precisely constructed context architecture that is deployed at the beginning of each session to re-establish the cognitive operating environment:

```
CORELEX™ INITIALIZATION BLOCK STRUCTURE:

[CORELEX™ ENVIRONMENT – SESSION INITIALIZATION]
```

```
PROJECT IDENTITY:
[Name and one-line description of the ongoing
work]

ANALYTICAL IDENTITY:
[Professional role, domain specialization,
analytical philosophy]
[Evidentiary standards that apply]
[Risk orientation and priority hierarchy]

TERMINOLOGY ARCHITECTURE:
[Key terms with precise operational definitions]
[Classification systems in use]
[Conceptual relationships that must be
maintained]

CONSTRAINT INHERITANCE:
[Operational constraints established in prior
sessions]
[Source boundaries in effect]
[Exclusion parameters]

CONTEXTUAL MOMENTUM:
[State of prior analytical work — what has been
established]
[Active hypotheses and unresolved threads]
[Next analytical objectives]

SESSION OBJECTIVE:
[Specific task for this session within the larger
project]

[CORELEX™ ENVIRONMENT ESTABLISHED — BEGIN]
```

This initialization block is not a prompt in the conventional sense. It is the reconstruction of a cognitive operating environment — the re-instantiation of an interpretive substrate that was active in prior sessions and is now being restored for the current one.

The operator who constructs and maintains a CoreLex environment across an extended project does something qualitatively different from the operator who re-explains their context at the beginning of each session. The former is maintaining a cognitive architecture. The latter is rebuilding one from scratch each time — a process that is not only inefficient but typically produces a degraded version of the original because memory is imperfect and context is always partially lost in the reconstruction.

2.8 The Evolution: From Static to Active to Persistent

Natural CodeLex positions CoreLex within a developmental trajectory of how the field has thought about contextual language environments in AI systems. This trajectory moves through three stages:

```
STAGE 1 – STATIC CORPUS ERA:
Corpora as passive repositories. Fixed
collections of text used for training,
benchmarking, and retrieval. The intelligence is
in the models trained on the corpus or the
algorithms that query it. The corpus itself is
inert.

Characteristic relationship: System → queries →
Corpus → returns → Information


STAGE 2 – DYNAMIC MEMORY ERA:
Memory systems as retrieval-oriented persistence.
Context windows, RAG, vector databases,
persistent chat memory. The system can access
prior information dynamically, but the
relationship remains fundamentally retrievalist:
find relevant stored information and inject it
into the active context.

Characteristic relationship: System → retrieves →
Memory → returns → Relevant information


STAGE 3 – COGNITIVE SUBSTRATE ERA (CoreLex):
Contextual environments as active cognition
architectures. The context is not a repository to
be queried but an environment to be inhabited.
The cognitive substrate shapes not just what
information is available but how the system
reasons – what analytical frameworks are active,
what interpretive postures govern generation,
what semantic architectures maintain continuity.
```

```
Characteristic relationship: System ↔ operates
within ↔ CoreLex Environment ↔ shapes ↔ Reasoning
behavior
```

The movement from Stage 1 to Stage 2 was primarily an engineering advance — better retrieval, larger memory, more sophisticated indexing. The movement from Stage 2 to Stage 3 is a conceptual advance — a reconceptualization of what the contextual environment is and what it should do.

Natural CodeLex does not claim to have built the technical infrastructure of Stage 3. Vector databases, context windows, and memory systems are engineering achievements that exist independently. What Natural CodeLex contributes is the architectural framework — the conceptual model for how these components can be orchestrated to create genuine cognitive substrate environments rather than sophisticated retrieval systems.

2.9 Future-State Implications: Where This Points

The CoreLex model points toward a future state in AI systems that is not yet fully realized but whose trajectory is becoming increasingly visible.

Current AI systems are fundamentally session-bounded. Each interaction begins fresh. The sophistication of the session depends entirely on what the operator constructs within it. Persistent memory systems add some continuity, but the cognitive architecture — the interpretive framework, the analytical posture, the semantic weighting system — must be reconstructed each time.

Future AI systems may move toward genuinely persistent contextual cognition environments — systems that maintain not just information but interpretive architecture across sessions, that develop and refine their analytical frameworks over time, that accumulate not just facts but reasoning sophistication within specific domains.

This future state would have profound implications for how AI is used in extended, complex work:

```
PERSISTENT ANALYTICAL ENVIRONMENTS:
```

> A legal team working with an AI system over months would not need to re-establish their analytical framework at the beginning of each session. The system would maintain their specific interpretive architecture – their risk thresholds, their precedent frameworks, their document classification systems – as a persistent cognitive environment that deepens rather than resets.
>
> EVOLVING COGNITIVE ARCHITECTURES:
> As work progresses and understanding develops, the CoreLex environment would evolve – incorporating new findings, refining analytical frameworks, updating conceptual maps. The system would become progressively more sophisticated within specific domains through accumulated cognitive architecture rather than just accumulated information.
>
> COLLABORATIVE COGNITIVE SUBSTRATES:
> Teams working with shared AI systems would share not just information but interpretive frameworks – a common cognitive substrate that ensures consistent analytical approaches, shared terminology, and coordinated reasoning across different team members' sessions.
>
> AGENTIC WORKFLOW CONTINUITY:
> AI agents engaged in extended autonomous work would maintain cognitive continuity across the full duration of a project – not just remembering what tasks they completed but maintaining the analytical frameworks and reasoning architectures through which they approached those tasks.

These future-state capabilities require both the engineering infrastructure to support persistent contextual environments and the architectural frameworks to design them well. CoreLex is Natural CodeLex's contribution to the second requirement — a conceptual model for what persistent cognitive substrates should preserve and how they should be structured.

2.10 What This Means for Operators Today

The full technical realization of persistent contextual cognition is a future state. The architectural principles are available to operators now — not because the technology has fully implemented them, but because disciplined operators can manually maintain CoreLex environments through the practices this framework describes.

Every time an operator constructs a dense initialization block that re-establishes their analytical framework at the beginning of a new session, they are manually implementing a CoreLex environment. Every time they maintain a compressed handoff document that preserves not just prior findings but the interpretive architecture through which those findings were reached, they are maintaining cognitive substrate continuity. Every time they invest in precise terminological definitions rather than assuming shared understanding, they are building a terminological architecture component of a CoreLex environment.

These practices are demanding. They require the operator to think explicitly about their cognitive architecture — to articulate not just what they want to accomplish but how they want to reason about it. This explicitness is both the cost and the benefit. The cost is the additional work of construction. The benefit is the compounding quality improvement of work conducted within a stable, coherent interpretive environment rather than a reconstructed one.

The operators who develop CoreLex maintenance as a discipline consistently report the same experience: work that would have required re-establishing context for hours at the beginning of each session instead begins immediately at the analytical frontier. The cognitive architecture is already in place. The system is already in the right analytical posture. The work can begin from where it left off rather than from the beginning.

Final Principle: Cognition, Not Just Memory

The evolution from corpus to memory to CoreLex is ultimately an evolution in what we understand the contextual environment of AI-mediated work to be.

Traditional corpora were collections. Memory systems are retrievers. CoreLex is a cognitive substrate — an active interpretive environment that shapes reasoning rather than merely supplying information.

The distinction matters because the most important thing that makes extended analytical work coherent is not the information available at any given moment but the interpretive framework through which that information is processed. Two analysts with access to identical information but operating within different interpretive frameworks will reach different conclusions, notice different patterns, and pursue different analytical directions. The framework is the cognition.

Natural CodeLex does not claim to have invented the components of this evolution. Corpora, memory systems, and retrieval architectures are established engineering achievements. What Natural CodeLex introduces through CoreLex is the synthesis — a unified architectural framework for thinking about contextual environments not as information repositories but as cognitive substrates, and for designing and maintaining those substrates in ways that preserve the most valuable and most fragile element of extended analytical work: the continuity of thought itself.

CHAPTER 3

THE AUTHORITY OF ITERATION

Why Strong AI Systems Emerge Through Refinement, Not Revelation

There is a fantasy embedded in how most people first approach AI systems. It is the fantasy of the perfect prompt — the idea that somewhere there exists a precise formulation that, if discovered, will produce ideal output reliably and immediately. Find the right words. Get the right answer. Move on.

This fantasy is not merely incorrect. It is operationally harmful. It orients the user toward a scavenger hunt for magic phrases rather than toward the systematic workflow discipline that actually produces high-quality AI outputs. It creates unrealistic expectations that lead to premature abandonment when first results disappoint. And it blinds users to the most powerful technique available to any AI operator: structured, deliberate, recursive iteration.

The authority of iteration is the principle that strong AI outputs almost always emerge through refinement rather than through single-pass generation — regardless of how sophisticated the initial prompt is. This is not a limitation of current AI capability that will be engineered away as models improve. It is a structural feature of probabilistic systems operating under interpretive uncertainty. Understanding why this is true, and how to act on it systematically, is one of the most important capabilities an AI operator can develop.

3.1 Why First Outputs Disappoint: The Mechanics

The first output of a complex AI task rarely represents the model's best capability. It represents the model's best guess under maximum interpretive uncertainty — the response that is most statistically plausible given the contextual information available at that moment.

When a prompt underspecifies the objective, the model faces a cascade of simultaneous inferential demands. It must determine not just what to say, but which of many possible analytical frameworks is most appropriate, what level of specificity the situation requires, what prior knowledge the operator already has, what organizational context is relevant, what tone and format will be most useful, and what the actual decision-driving question behind the surface request actually is.

Under this inferential load, the model typically produces one of three first-output failure patterns:

> OVERGENERALIZATION: The model selects the broadest plausible interpretation and generates output applicable across all contexts – which means specifically useful for none. A strategic analysis prompt returns a textbook overview of strategic analysis frameworks. A risk assessment prompt returns a generic catalog of risk categories. The output is technically correct and operationally inert.
>
> MISALIGNMENT: The model correctly interprets the surface request but emphasizes the wrong variables. Asked to analyze operational inefficiencies, it focuses on cost savings when the actual concern is customer retention. Asked to assess market risk, it emphasizes macroeconomic factors when the actual concern is competitive dynamics. The output addresses the question asked rather than the need behind it.
>
> FALSE CONFIDENCE: The model generates fluent, structured, authoritative-sounding output that contains incorrect assumptions, unsupported inferences, or reasoning errors presented with uniform confidence. The professional appearance of the output obscures its analytical fragility. This is the most dangerous first-output failure because it is the hardest to detect without specific adversarial review.

Advanced operators do not interpret these failure patterns as evidence of model inadequacy. They interpret them as calibration data — diagnostic information about the gap between what was specified and what was needed. The first output reveals the model's default assumptions and interpretive tendencies. Iteration then corrects alignment by closing that gap systematically.

3.2 A Complete Iterative Workflow: Step by Step

Abstract principles become real through demonstration. The following shows a complete iterative workflow applied to a genuine enterprise analysis problem — tracking every prompt, diagnosing every output pattern, and documenting the refinement logic at each stage.

```
PROBLEM: A healthcare technology company needs to
understand why customer retention is declining
among small hospital systems (50-200 beds) in the
first 18 months after EHR implementation.

ROUND 1 – INITIAL PROMPT:
'Analyze why customer retention might be
declining after EHR implementation.'

OUTPUT PATTERN: Generic survey of retention
factors across all healthcare IT contexts. Covers
training adequacy, technical support quality,
integration complexity, user adoption, and
contract structure – all at identical shallow
depth. No prioritization. No segment specificity.
Could apply to any healthcare IT product in any
decade.

DIAGNOSIS: Objective dramatically underspecified.
No segment defined. No timeframe specified. No
organizational context. Model defaulted to
maximum-breadth statistical average.

WHAT THIS TELLS US: Model's default interpretive
frame for 'EHR retention decline' is a generic
healthcare IT problem. Our actual problem is
specific to small hospital systems in the 18-
month post-implementation window.

ROUND 2 – REFINEMENT 1:
IDENTITY: Senior customer success strategist
specializing in healthcare IT for community
hospitals.
OBJECTIVE: Identify retention failure drivers
specific to small hospital systems (50-200 beds)
in months 6-18 post-EHR implementation.
```

EXCLUDE: Technical support quality (already assessed — not the primary driver). Contract structure issues (sales problem, not retention problem).

OUTPUT: Ranked failure drivers by retention impact.

OUTPUT PATTERN: Substantially better. Now addresses workflow disruption, physician adoption resistance, and administrative staff turnover specifically. Some specificity around the 6–18 month window. Still somewhat generic within each category — describes problems without operational specificity.

DIAGNOSIS: Segment and timeframe constraints working. Identity framing activated domain-relevant vocabulary. Gaps: analytical depth still surface-level. Needs operational specificity within each failure driver.

ROUND 3 — REFINEMENT 2:

For each failure driver identified, provide:

- The specific operational mechanism producing the failure
- Observable behavioral symptoms that would appear in customer data
- The typical trigger event or timeline within the 6–18 month window
- One intervention approach with documented effectiveness in analogous cases

OUTPUT PATTERN: Significantly denser. Physician adoption resistance now broken into three distinct mechanisms with specific trigger timelines. Administrative staff turnover linked to specific workflow burden patterns measurable in usage data. Intervention approaches concrete rather than generic.

DIAGNOSIS: Approaching target quality. One remaining gap: claims about 'documented effectiveness' are asserted without evidence basis — confidence miscalibration risk.

ROUND 4 — ADVERSARIAL REVIEW:

Challenge the previous analysis directly. For each finding:

```
- Identify whether the evidentiary basis is
strong, moderate, or speculative
- Identify one alternative explanation that the
analysis may be underweighting
- Flag any assumption that, if wrong, would
significantly change the conclusion

FINAL OUTPUT: Findings maintained with explicit
confidence levels. Three assumptions flagged for
validation. One alternative explanation surfaced
(administrative burden may be symptom of
physician resistance rather than independent
driver). Analysis is now decision-ready with
appropriate epistemic transparency.

OUTCOME: Four rounds produced output that no
initial prompt could have generated — not because
the model became more capable, but because the
interpretive environment was progressively
clarified through structured refinement.
```

This is iterative authority in practice. The power is not in any individual prompt. It is in the systematic architecture of progressive clarification — each round closing the gap between what was specified and what was needed, building on what worked and correcting what did not.

3.3 The Iteration Taxonomy

Not all iteration serves the same purpose. Applying the wrong type of iteration to a workflow problem is as inefficient as applying no iteration at all. Natural CodeLex identifies six functionally distinct forms of iteration, each targeting a specific alignment gap:

```
COMPRESSION ITERATION
Purpose: Increase signal density by removing
redundancy and narrative padding.
When to use: Output is accurate and appropriately
scoped but verbose — contains the right content
at too much length with too much filler.
Method: Increase analytical density. Remove
narrative padding. Prioritize finding statements
over explanatory elaboration.
Example refinement prompt: 'Compress the previous
analysis. Remove transitional prose and
introductory framing. Keep findings, discard
```

explanation of findings. Target 40% of current length.'

ADVERSARIAL ITERATION
Purpose: Surface blind spots, challenge unsupported conclusions, and identify alternative interpretations.
When to use: Output appears confident and well-structured but has not been challenged. Risk of false confidence failure mode.
Method: Directly challenge conclusions. Identify unsupported assumptions. Request alternative explanations.
Example refinement prompt: 'Challenge every conclusion in the previous analysis. For each finding, identify one plausible alternative explanation and one assumption that, if wrong, invalidates the finding.'

IDENTITY ITERATION
Purpose: Reframe analysis through a more appropriate professional perspective.
When to use: Output lacks domain-specific depth or emphasizes the wrong analytical dimensions for the actual decision context.
Method: Assign a more specific professional identity and re-run the analysis.
Example refinement prompt: 'Re-analyze this problem as a forensic compliance auditor rather than a general consultant. What risks does that lens reveal that the previous analysis missed?'

CONSTRAINT ITERATION
Purpose: Narrow interpretive space when output remains too broad or is covering irrelevant territory.
When to use: Output continues to address variables outside the actual target scope despite earlier scope instructions.
Method: Add explicit exclusion constraints. Reinforce scope boundaries. Add structural format requirements that prevent scope drift.
Example refinement prompt: 'The previous analysis continued to address marketing factors. Exclude all marketing considerations entirely. Reanalyze for operational factors only. If a finding has a marketing component, omit it.'

```
VERIFICATION ITERATION
Purpose: Improve epistemic reliability by
identifying unverified claims and confidence
miscalibration.
When to use: Output contains confident assertions
that require validation, or treats speculative
inferences as established conclusions.
Method: Request explicit confidence levels. Ask
for evidentiary basis for specific claims. Flag
claims requiring external verification.
Example refinement prompt: 'For each factual
claim in the previous analysis, indicate whether
the basis is: (a) directly derivable from
provided source material, (b) reasonable
inference from provided material, or (c) general
knowledge assumption. Flag all (c) claims for
external verification.'

SYNTHESIS ITERATION
Purpose: Compress multiple rounds of output into
a unified, decision-ready format.
When to use: Multiple rounds have produced
diverse, sometimes conflicting findings that need
to be integrated into a single coherent output.
Method: Provide previous outputs as input.
Instruct synthesis toward specific decision
format.
Example refinement prompt: 'Synthesize the
findings from the three previous analyses into a
single prioritized recommendation. Where findings
conflict, explain the conflict and your
resolution rationale. Target format: executive
decision brief, maximum 400 words.'
```

Understanding which type of iteration a workflow needs is itself an advanced skill. The operator who applies adversarial iteration to an output that needs compression, or compression iteration to an output that needs verification, will make progress slowly. The operator who correctly diagnoses the specific gap and applies the appropriate iteration type compounds improvement rapidly.

3.4 Iteration as Cognitive Calibration

One of the most useful conceptual frames for understanding iteration is cognitive calibration — the progressive narrowing of the model's interpretive range through successive contextual specification.

Each refinement cycle accomplishes two things simultaneously. First, it improves the model's alignment with the operator's actual intent by providing additional architectural guidance. Second — and this is underappreciated — it often reveals previously hidden assumptions in the operator's own thinking.

Many operators discover through the iteration process that their initial request was underspecified not because they forgot to include details, but because they had not yet fully clarified their own objectives. The process of constructing a refinement prompt forces a kind of analytical precision that the initial request did not require. What specifically is wrong with this output? What is it doing that it should not be doing? What is it missing that it should include? Answering these questions requires the operator to articulate the actual target with a specificity that often was not present in the initial request.

In this sense, the AI system functions partly as a reflective surface — a mechanism that exposes the quality of human thinking through the quality of its responses. Vague outputs are often signals of vague objectives. Misaligned outputs are often signals of underspecified targets. System failures illuminate operator assumptions — a diagnostic value independent of output utility.

This dynamic is why experienced AI operators consistently report that their ability to formulate initial prompts improves substantially over time. The feedback loop between prompt quality and output quality creates a learning system — the operator who iterates thoughtfully becomes more precise in their initial framing because they have developed, through practice, a clearer model of what specification produces what output.

3.5 Enterprise Parallels: Red Teams, Legal Review, Editorial Process

Iterative refinement is not a novel AI concept invented by prompt engineers. It mirrors review architectures that high-stakes organizations have used for decades — architectures that exist precisely because single-pass generation of complex outputs is reliably insufficient for consequential decisions.

Military red-teaming has been a standard element of operational planning since at least World War II. The practice assigns adversarial analysts — the 'red team' — to challenge operational plans before execution, with the explicit mandate to find failure modes that the planning team has normalized or missed. The red team's value comes from their externality to the planning process: they have not been through the same iterations that made specific assumptions feel obvious to the planners, so they can see what the planners have stopped seeing. The structural logic is identical to adversarial iteration in AI workflows — the value comes from forcing a challenge to conclusions that have not yet been challenged.

Legal review chains operate on the same multi-pass logic. A significant contract typically passes through drafting, internal business review, internal legal review, external counsel review, compliance review, and executive sign-off. Each layer targets a different class of risk: business review surfaces commercial structure issues, legal review surfaces liability issues, compliance review surfaces regulatory issues, executive review surfaces strategic issues. The redundancy is not inefficiency — it is risk architecture. The assumption is that no single reviewer catches every class of problem, and that the cost of missed problems in executed contracts significantly exceeds the cost of multi-layer review.

Editorial processes in serious publishing follow the same structural logic. A manuscript passes through developmental editing (does the overall structure work?), line editing (does the argument flow coherently?), copy editing (is the language precise and consistent?), and proofreading (are there surface errors?). Each stage targets a different quality dimension. Authors who skip stages typically produce weaker books regardless of their talent — not because any single stage is irreplaceable, but because each stage catches problems that the others are not optimized to find.

Advanced AI iteration is not a simulation of these processes. It is the compression of their structural logic into a single workflow operating at dramatically higher speed. The iterative AI workflow does in minutes what legal review chains and editorial processes do in days or weeks — not as well, but with the same underlying principle: that complex outputs become reliable through structured successive review, not through single-pass generation regardless of how sophisticated the initial attempt.

3.6 Signal Density and Attention Allocation

One important reason iteration improves outputs involves the relationship between signal density and attentional allocation.

Language models distribute attention dynamically across contextual inputs. Well-specified prompts create clear attentional hierarchies — the model can reliably identify which elements are most important and allocate generative capacity accordingly. Poorly specified prompts create attentional ambiguity — the model must guess at importance hierarchies, often defaulting to treating all inputs as roughly equal, which means that low-priority elements receive the same attentional weight as high-priority ones.

Iteration addresses this through progressive specificity. Each refinement cycle typically either increases signal density (by removing low-value content and reinforcing high-value content) or restructures attentional hierarchy (by explicitly labeling priorities, adding structural formatting that signals importance, or removing competing signals that distract from the actual target).

The practical result is that iterated prompts often work better not because they contain more information, but because they contain better-organized information — information structured so that the model can reliably identify what matters most and spend its generative capacity there.

3.7 Adversarial Iteration: The Most Powerful Technique

Among the six iteration types, adversarial iteration is both the most powerful and the most underused. It deserves extended treatment because its benefits are not intuitive and its application requires deliberate effort.

The core problem that adversarial iteration addresses is narrative momentum — the tendency of language models to continue reinforcing the analytical direction established in their initial response. Once the model has committed to a particular framing of a problem, subsequent generation within that session tends to elaborate, extend, and defend that framing rather than challenge it. The model is not being stubborn or defensive. It is doing exactly what probabilistic generation predicts: the established narrative creates contextual pressure toward consistent continuation.

Adversarial iteration interrupts this momentum by explicitly changing the generative target. Instead of asking for elaboration on existing conclusions, it asks for challenges to them. This reorients the probability distribution away from 'what is consistent with what I have already said' and toward 'what is inconsistent with it' — a fundamentally different generative task that surfaces a fundamentally different class of information.

The practical impact is substantial. In systematic tests across analytical tasks, outputs that have been subjected to adversarial iteration contain significantly fewer unsupported assumptions, show better calibrated confidence, and produce more resilient conclusions than outputs that have not been challenged. The mechanism is not magical — it is structural. Forcing the model to find problems with its own conclusions is more likely to surface those problems than continuing to elaborate on them.

A practical adversarial prompt structure that consistently produces results:

```
ADVERSARIAL REVIEW INSTRUCTION:
```

```
Challenge the previous analysis rigorously. Your
goal is to find problems, not confirm strengths.

For each major conclusion or recommendation:
1. Identify the primary assumption it depends on
2. Identify one plausible scenario in which that
assumption fails
3. Identify one alternative explanation that the
analysis underweighted or ignored
4. Rate the overall evidentiary support as:
Strong / Moderate / Speculative

Do not preserve diplomatic framing. The goal is
accuracy, not comfort.
Flag any claim where you cannot identify clear
supporting evidence from the provided material.
```

The instruction explicitly licenses the model to be critical — which matters because models are trained on human feedback that tends to reward agreement and helpfulness. Without explicit permission to challenge, the model's default tendency is toward affirmation rather than critique. The adversarial prompt reorients that default.

3.8 Iterative Failure Modes

Iteration is not automatically beneficial. Poorly managed iterative workflows can degrade output quality through specific failure modes that operators should anticipate and design against.

```
CONTEXTUAL INSTABILITY: The operator repeatedly
modifies objectives across refinement rounds
without maintaining coherent priorities. Each
round introduces new constraints or goals that
partially contradict earlier ones. The model
begins responding inconsistently because the
contextual hierarchy has become genuinely
ambiguous – there is no longer a clear answer to
'what does this operator actually want?' The
outputs become harder to evaluate because the
target keeps shifting.

CONTRADICTORY CONSTRAINTS: Successive refinements
introduce instructions that cannot be
simultaneously satisfied. 'Be comprehensive' and
'be concise.' 'Cover all relevant factors' and
```

```
'limit to three findings.' 'Maintain analytical
depth' and 'use plain language for a general
audience.' The model attempts parallel
satisfaction of incompatible requirements and
produces output that inadequately satisfies all
of them.

RECURSION COLLAPSE: Excessive iteration without
compression produces diminishing returns as the
context window fills with accumulated revision
history. The signal from productive earlier
refinements becomes diluted by the volume of
subsequent exchanges. Output quality plateaus or
declines even as the number of iterations
increases. The session has become too long and
too complex to sustain focus.

HALLUCINATION AMPLIFICATION: An incorrect
assumption enters the workflow early and is
reinforced through successive iterations. Each
round builds on the flawed premise, making it
more deeply embedded and more coherent-sounding.
By the fifth or sixth iteration, the
hallucination has been elaborated into a highly
structured, apparently well-reasoned conclusion
that originated from a factual error. Adversarial
iteration and periodic source verification are
the primary defenses against this pattern.
```

Strong iteration requires architectural discipline. Each refinement cycle should have a specific diagnostic target, preserve objective clarity, and move toward structural coherence rather than away from it. When a workflow shows signs of any of these failure modes, the correct response is usually compression and reset — synthesizing current progress into a clean handoff block and starting a fresh session with clearer architecture — rather than continuing to iterate within a degraded context.

3.9 Iteration and Human Thinking

One of the consistently underappreciated consequences of disciplined AI iteration is its effect on the operator's thinking, independent of the AI outputs it produces.

Constructing an adversarial review prompt requires the operator to articulate what a strong critique of their own analysis would look like — which requires having thought carefully enough about the analysis to identify its potential weaknesses. Constructing a constraint iteration prompt requires the operator to identify precisely what is wrong with the current output — which requires knowing specifically enough what they want to distinguish it from what they got. Constructing a synthesis prompt requires the operator to clarify what the decision-relevant conclusions are — which requires having a clear enough view of the actual decision to prioritize findings accordingly.

In each case, the act of constructing the refinement prompt demands cognitive work that produces value independent of what the model returns. The operator who iterates thoughtfully develops, through the process, a more precise understanding of their own problem, their own objectives, and the structure of their own analytical uncertainty.

This is one reason that sophisticated AI users consistently report that working with AI systems has made them better thinkers — not just more productive ones. The iterative loop is not just a technique for improving AI outputs. It is a feedback system that progressively trains operators toward greater analytical precision, more explicit hypothesis formation, and more disciplined epistemic habits.

Final Principle: Iteration as Architecture

The authority of iteration is not about endlessly rewriting prompts until the model produces the desired answer through attrition. It is about understanding that strong AI workflows emerge through structured, purposeful refinement — each round targeting a specific alignment gap with a specific type of iterative intervention.

Large language models are probabilistic synthesis engines operating under interpretive uncertainty. Their outputs improve when that uncertainty is progressively reduced through architectural refinement. The most capable AI operators are not the ones who write the most impressive initial prompts. They are the ones who iterate most intelligently — who diagnose output failures accurately, apply the right type of iteration efficiently, and know when to compress and reset rather than continuing to elaborate within a degrading context.

Advanced prompting is not ultimately about commanding machines. It is about building iterative cognitive environments capable of producing increasingly stable, useful, and strategically aligned outcomes through the kind of structured successive refinement that high-stakes human review architectures have relied on for decades.

CHAPTER 4

CONTEXT IS THE REAL OPERATING SYSTEM

The Architecture of Attention

Ask ten AI users what the most important factor in getting good outputs is, and nine will say the prompt. They will talk about word choice, specificity, clarity of instruction — all legitimate considerations. They are looking at the right landscape but focusing on the wrong feature.

The prompt is the most visible layer of the interaction. It is what the operator consciously constructs and explicitly controls. But the prompt does not operate in isolation. It operates within a context — a broader informational environment that shapes how the model interprets every instruction, weights every constraint, and selects among the enormous range of possible continuations available to it.

Context is the actual operating system of AI performance. The prompt is an application running on top of it. A well-written application on a corrupted operating system produces corrupted outputs. A modest application on a clean, well-configured operating system often produces remarkably good results. The implication is direct: operators who focus exclusively on individual prompt quality while neglecting contextual architecture are optimizing the wrong layer.

This chapter develops a systematic understanding of context — how it works, how it degrades, how it can be designed and maintained, and what it means for serious AI workflows at individual and organizational scale.

4.1 What Context Actually Is

In everyday usage, 'context' often means background information — the surrounding circumstances that help explain something. In AI systems, context has a more precise and operationally important meaning.

The context window is the complete set of information available to the model at the moment of generation. It includes everything: the current prompt, the entire conversation history of the session, any documents or reference material that have been uploaded, system-level instructions, and the accumulated residue of every prior exchange.

Every element of this context window simultaneously influences the generation process. The model does not process the current prompt in isolation, refer to prior context when needed, and then set it aside. It processes the entire context window as an integrated input, with every element exerting influence proportional to its attentional salience. Prior conversation shapes how current instructions are interpreted. Accumulated stylistic patterns shape the probability distribution of current generation. Established concepts and framing persist and influence analysis even when not explicitly invoked.

This means that two operators sending the identical prompt to the same model may receive substantially different outputs if the contextual environments surrounding that prompt differ. A request for a formal risk analysis sent in the context of twenty exchanges about risk management will produce a different output than the identical request sent in the context of twenty exchanges about creative brainstorming — not because the prompt changed, but because the operating environment changed.

Most users encounter this dynamic as mysterious inconsistency: why does the AI sometimes respond brilliantly to a prompt and other times poorly to what seems like the same request? The answer is almost always context. The request is not the same. The contextual environment in which it is embedded has changed.

4.2 Context Contamination: A Case Study

Nothing illustrates the operational reality of context better than a concrete demonstration of context contamination — the failure mode in which accumulated contextual residue from incompatible tasks degrades analytical quality in ways that are invisible unless the operator understands what is happening.

Consider the following session progression:

```
SESSION ARCHITECTURE — A CONTAMINATION CASE

HOURS 1-2: FORENSIC CONTRACT REVIEW
Operator establishes: Identity as legal auditor.
Objective: liability exposure analysis. Output:
risk-ranked findings. Source constraint: document
only.

Model behavior: Strong, precise outputs. Dense
legal language. Specific clause identification.
Conservative evidentiary standards. Appropriate
hedging on speculative inferences. Exactly what
was designed.

HOUR 2 — TOPIC SHIFT:
Operator asks: 'What do you think about the
culture problems we discussed with the leadership
team?'
Few exchanges of conversational analysis follow —
informal, exploratory, somewhat emotional in
tone.

HOUR 2.5 — SECOND TOPIC SHIFT:
Operator asks: 'Can you help me draft a message
to the team about these challenges? Make it
inspiring.'
Several rounds of collaborative drafting follow —
warm, narrative, motivational in style.

HOUR 3 — RETURN TO ORIGINAL TASK:
Operator: 'Continue the contract risk analysis we
were doing earlier.'

OUTPUT COMPARISON:

BEFORE CONTAMINATION (Hour 1-2 output sample):
```

```
'Section 14.3 creates asymmetric indemnification
obligations that expose the counterparty to
unlimited liability for third-party claims
arising from data processing activities. This
creates material legal risk that should be
negotiated prior to execution.'

AFTER CONTAMINATION (Hour 3 output sample):
'Section 14.3 addresses indemnification in ways
that raise some questions worth exploring
together as a team. The language around data
processing could potentially create challenges,
and it might be worth having a conversation with
stakeholders about how to navigate these dynamics
thoughtfully.'

NOTE: Both outputs address the same clause. The
analytical substance has not changed. But the
language, the confidence, the precision, and the
professional posture have degraded dramatically.
The model is still processing legal content
through a warm, collaborative, stakeholder-
management lens established three hours earlier.
```

The user experiences this as: 'The AI stopped being rigorous.' The actual problem is not model failure — it is contextual pollution. The session accumulated incompatible operational trajectories and blended them together in ways that corrupted the specific behavioral profile the operator needed.

This failure is invisible to operators who do not understand context architecture. They conclude that AI is unreliable. The actual conclusion is that contextual management is a required skill, not an optional one.

4.3 A Real Failure: The Collapsed Compliance Review

The following is a composite drawn from documented enterprise AI deployment patterns. It is representative, not hypothetical.

A mid-sized professional services firm deployed AI for contract compliance review across its legal operations team. In the first month, results were strong. The AI, operating within a carefully constructed compliance identity with source-bound constraints and formal output requirements, produced risk-ranked contract analyses that senior counsel described as genuinely useful.

By month three, quality had degraded significantly. The legal team could not explain why.

The cause was textbook context contamination at organizational scale. The firm had not segmented its AI usage by function. The same environment was used for contract review in the morning, communication drafting at midday, strategic brainstorming in the afternoon, and client notes at end of day. Each use case accumulated in the shared context. By the time attorneys returned to contract review the following morning, they were often continuing sessions contaminated by twelve hours of incompatible contextual residue.

The outputs still looked like compliance analyses — same structure, similar length. But risk language had softened. Conservative evidentiary standards had given way to diplomatic hedging. The adversarial posture essential for genuine liability assessment had been replaced by something closer to stakeholder communication tone.

Nobody caught it immediately because the outputs still read as professional. The Coherence Trap held. It took a near-miss on a contract with a significant asymmetric indemnification clause — flagged correctly by outside counsel, missed by the AI review — to trigger a forensic analysis of the workflow. The fix was architectural: separate sessions per domain, front-loaded context stacks, Context Fencing between tasks. Quality recovered within two weeks.

4.4 The Context Stack Architecture

If context is the operating system of AI performance, then the operator needs a framework for designing and maintaining it deliberately rather than allowing it to accumulate accidentally. Natural CodeLex introduces the Context Stack for exactly this purpose.

The Context Stack is a layered architecture of operational parameters that defines the model's behavioral environment across six functional dimensions. Each layer serves a distinct purpose, and their alignment determines the overall quality of the contextual environment.

```
LAYER 1 — IDENTITY LAYER
Definition: Who is the model operating as? What
professional perspective, domain expertise, and
analytical posture should dominate?
Function: Activates domain-specific language
patterns, analytical frameworks, and epistemic
standards associated with the specified
professional identity.
Example: 'Identity: Senior enterprise risk
auditor specializing in operational compliance
for financial services institutions.'
What it affects: Vocabulary selection, risk
threshold calibration, evidentiary standards,
output formality, analytical priorities.

LAYER 2 — OBJECTIVE LAYER
Definition: What must be accomplished? What
operational goal does the output serve?
Function: Narrows the interpretive target and
defines what success looks like beyond the
surface request.
Example: 'Objective: Identify compliance exposure
that could trigger regulatory action in a
scheduled examination — not general risk
awareness.'
What it affects: Analytical focus, depth of
treatment per finding, prioritization criteria,
output usefulness for the actual decision.

LAYER 3 — MEMORY LAYER
Definition: What established context from prior
sessions or prior exchanges is operationally
relevant to this task?
Function: Maintains analytical continuity without
requiring raw conversation history to be carried
into new sessions.
Example: 'Prior context: Analysis in prior
session established that data governance is the
highest-priority risk domain. Treat this as
established — do not re-examine it. Focus on
second-tier risks.'
```

What it affects: Analytical starting point, avoidance of re-covering established ground, session efficiency.

LAYER 4 – CONSTRAINT LAYER

Definition: What should be avoided, excluded, or bounded?

Function: Defines the negative space – the behaviors and content that should not appear – which is as important as positive specification.

Example: 'Constraints: No speculation beyond documented evidence. No general risk awareness findings – only findings with specific regulatory exposure. No marketing or reputational risk – operational and compliance only.'

What it affects: Output relevance, scope discipline, hallucination risk, analytical precision.

LAYER 5 – OUTPUT LAYER

Definition: What does a successful result look like structurally?

Function: Anchors the generative process to a specific deliverable format, preventing format drift and ensuring the output is usable in the intended context.

Example: 'Output: Ranked risk matrix. Each item: risk description, regulatory basis, severity rating (Critical/High/Medium), and recommended remediation priority.'

What it affects: Output usability, consistency across sessions, ease of review and application.

LAYER 6 – VERIFICATION LAYER

Definition: How will quality be assessed? What epistemic standards must the output meet?

Function: Embeds quality control into the generative instruction itself rather than leaving it to post-generation review.

Example: 'Verification: Each finding must be tied to a specific provision in the provided documentation. Flag any finding that relies on inference rather than explicit text. Assign confidence levels.'

What it affects: Analytical reliability, hallucination detection, epistemic transparency.

When all six layers are explicitly defined and coherently aligned, the Context Stack creates a highly stable operational environment in which the model's behavioral distribution is narrowed dramatically toward the intended target. When layers are absent, inconsistent, or internally conflicting, the model fills the gaps with statistical defaults — which means the operator's actual needs are addressed only to the extent they overlap with the average across all similar requests.

The difference between a well-constructed Context Stack and no Context Stack is not marginal. It is often the difference between outputs that require significant revision before use and outputs that are deployment-ready.

4.5 Context Fencing

Context contamination occurs because AI sessions operate as integrated environments — everything that enters the context window influences everything that follows. Context Fencing is the deliberate practice of preventing this contamination by creating explicit operational boundaries.

The principle is straightforward: tasks that require incompatible contextual environments should not share the same session. Legal analysis and creative brainstorming should not be in the same context. Technical forensic review and motivational communication drafting should not be in the same context. Strategic planning and casual organizational discussion should not be in the same context.

When task separation is not possible within a single session — because of workflow requirements or time constraints — Context Fencing establishes explicit boundary markers:

```
CONTEXT FENCE INSTRUCTION:

[CONTEXT BOUNDARY]

Previous discussion of team dynamics and
communication is now closed. Do not carry forward
any stylistic, tonal, or analytical patterns from
that discussion.

New operating context:
```

```
IDENTITY: Forensic compliance auditor
OBJECTIVE: Technical risk extraction from
provided documentation
TONE: Formal, precise, conservative
STYLE: Source-bound, evidence-cited, no narrative
elaboration

Previous context influence: None. Start fresh
from the established identity and constraints
above.

[CONTEXT BOUNDARY ESTABLISHED]
```

The explicit boundary instruction signals a deliberate reset of the operational context. It does not eliminate the prior context from the window — the model still has access to it — but it establishes a strong attentional signal that the prior context should not shape the current task. Combined with a clearly re-established Context Stack, this instruction typically produces a substantial recovery of analytical precision even within a contaminated session.

4.6 Shadow Context

Among the contextual phenomena that affect AI outputs, Shadow Context is perhaps the most subtle and the most underappreciated.

Shadow Context refers to the accumulated atmospheric residue of a session — the implicit tonal, emotional, and stylistic patterns established through prior exchanges that influence generation even when not explicitly referenced.

Consider a session that has spent twenty exchanges analyzing organizational failure, crisis management, reputational damage, and executive accountability. The explicit content of those exchanges is obviously present in the context window. But something less obvious is also present: a persistent atmospheric orientation toward threat, consequence, and high-stakes judgment. This orientation functions as Shadow Context — it colors the probability distribution of subsequent generation in ways that are difficult to trace back to any specific prior exchange.

A model that has been operating in this atmospheric context may generate more cautious, hedge-heavy, risk-emphasizing outputs on subsequent tasks — not because the operator asked for caution, but because the probability distribution has been persistently shifted toward risk-conscious language patterns by the accumulated context.

Similarly, a session heavy with motivational language, aspirational framing, and collaborative tone will generate subsequent outputs that carry that warmth and optimism — even when the subsequent task calls for adversarial analysis or conservative risk assessment.

Shadow Context is not about conscious model 'mood' — the model has no emotional states. It is about statistical momentum: the contextual atmosphere established through prior exchanges shifts the probability distribution of subsequent generation in systematic and detectable ways. Advanced operators learn to monitor this shift and reset when it threatens to contaminate operationally important tasks.

4.7 Enterprise Context Segmentation

The context contamination problem, challenging at the individual level, becomes operationally critical at enterprise scale. Organizations that attempt to use AI across multiple functional domains within shared or insufficiently segmented contextual environments consistently encounter performance degradation that they attribute to model limitations rather than architectural failures.

Consider the cross-domain contamination problem systematically:

```
ENTERPRISE CONTAMINATION SCENARIO

Domain 1 — Legal/Compliance:
Required contextual environment: Conservative,
cautious, source-bound, risk-escalating, formally
precise.
If contaminated by: Creative, exploratory, or
motivational content → analysis becomes
```

```
underqualified, overly approachable, risk-
minimizing.

Domain 2 — Creative/Marketing:
Required contextual environment: Exploratory,
generative, narratively fluid, audience-
empathetic.
If contaminated by: Legal/compliance content →
outputs become defensive, over-qualified, legally
hedged in ways that undermine persuasive impact.

Domain 3 — Financial Analysis:
Required contextual environment: Numerically
precise, conservative in assumptions, evidence-
bound, model-specific.
If contaminated by: Strategic or narrative
content → outputs become qualitative and
directional rather than quantitative and
specific.

Domain 4 — Strategic Planning:
Required contextual environment: Hypothesis-
generative, directionally ambitious, comfortable
with uncertainty.
If contaminated by: Compliance content → strategy
becomes overly conservative, opportunity-
minimizing, risk-dominated.

Each domain requires a contextual environment
that actively conflicts with the others.
Operating them in shared sessions produces
outputs that inadequately serve all domains
simultaneously.
```

The architectural response is contextual segmentation — treating each functional domain as a distinct operational environment with its own Context Stack, its own session architecture, and its own clean starting conditions. This mirrors the principle of environment isolation in software engineering: development, staging, and production environments are separated precisely because their operational requirements conflict, and contamination across environments produces failures in all of them.

The strongest enterprise AI implementations increasingly recognize that the value is not in having a single powerful AI system available across all functions. The value is in having function-specific contextual architectures that allow each domain to operate at full quality within its appropriate behavioral environment.

4.8 Context Windows, Capacity, and Curation

Modern AI systems offer context windows of substantial size — enough to hold the equivalent of multiple lengthy documents, extended conversation histories, and complex analytical frameworks simultaneously. This capacity has led to a widespread and operationally harmful assumption: that larger context equals better performance, and that filling the context window is always beneficial.

This assumption is false in ways that matter practically.

A large context window filled with conflicting instructions, redundant information, accumulated conversational noise, and irrelevant material produces degraded outputs — often worse than a smaller context window with a well-curated, high-density set of relevant information. The capacity for large context does not change the fundamental economics of attention: signal and noise compete for the same attentional resources, and as noise increases, signal quality decreases.

The implication is that effective context management is not about maximizing context volume. It is about curating context quality — maintaining the informational elements that contribute to alignment while actively removing or isolating the elements that create noise.

This curation requires deliberate effort. It means resisting the temptation to upload all available reference material when only specific sections are relevant. It means starting fresh sessions rather than continuing to extend conversations that have accumulated significant noise. It means constructing compressed handoff blocks that carry forward only the operationally necessary elements of prior work rather than pasting raw conversation history.

Context is valuable. More context is not automatically more valuable. Better-organized context is almost always more valuable than more context.

4.9 Context Resetting and Maintenance

Context degradation is not a one-time event — it is a continuous process. Every exchange that enters a session adds new material to the contextual environment, creating new attentional competition, potentially introducing new tonal or stylistic residue, and gradually diluting the influence of constraints and objectives established earlier in the session.

Advanced operators therefore treat context management as an ongoing maintenance discipline rather than a one-time setup task. This maintenance takes two primary forms.

Periodic reinforcement involves re-establishing critical constraints and objectives within a long session at regular intervals — not because the model has forgotten them, but because their attentional salience has declined as new context has entered the window. A brief constraint reinforcement block every ten to fifteen exchanges in a complex session maintains alignment without requiring a full reset:

```
PERIODIC REINFORCEMENT BLOCK:

REMINDER – Operating constraints remain:
- Source-bound reasoning only
- Forensic audit identity – not advisory
- Risk-ranked output format
- No speculation beyond documented evidence

Continue from previous analysis.
```

Session resetting involves deliberately ending a contaminated or overly long session and beginning fresh with a well-constructed Context Stack and a compressed handoff block carrying only the operationally necessary prior findings. This is not a retreat — it is architectural maintenance. Just as software systems require periodic maintenance to prevent complexity accumulation from degrading performance, AI sessions require periodic resetting to prevent contextual accumulation from degrading output quality.

The operator who refuses to reset because it feels like losing progress is typically sacrificing output quality for the psychological comfort of session continuity. The output quality loss from operating in a heavily contaminated context almost always exceeds whatever efficiency gains the apparent continuity provides.

Final Principle: Context Is Infrastructure

Context is the hidden operating system behind AI performance. The prompt alone is rarely the entire story. Outputs are shaped by surrounding information, prior instructions, contextual residue, structural organization, and attentional allocation in ways that are invisible to operators who focus exclusively on individual prompt quality.

Weak context creates drift, instability, hallucination risk, and inconsistent outputs. Strong context — deliberately designed, actively maintained, and appropriately segmented — creates alignment, clarity, operational focus, and improved reasoning consistency across extended workflows.

The future of advanced AI usage will not belong to the operators writing the most dramatic prompts. It will belong to the operators designing the strongest contextual environments — because context is not background. Context is infrastructure. And infrastructure quality determines what is possible to build on top of it.

CHAPTER 5

CONSTRAINTS CREATE INTELLIGENCE

Why Boundaries Improve AI Performance

The most counterintuitive principle in Natural CodeLex is this: freedom often weakens AI output quality, and constraint often improves it.

This principle runs directly against the dominant intuition that most users bring to AI systems. The prevailing assumption is that the best way to engage a powerful AI is to give it maximum latitude — to be open-ended, to avoid restrictions, to let the system exercise its full capability without artificial limits. This assumption produces some of the weakest AI outputs available, for reasons that become clear once the mechanics of probabilistic generation are understood.

Large language models generate outputs by navigating an enormous probability space. Every generation decision involves selecting among thousands of possible continuations, with the selection governed by the probability distribution created by the contextual inputs. When that context provides minimal guidance — when prompts are vague, broad, and unconstrained — the probability space remains vast, and the model navigates it by defaulting to statistical averages: the most common combinations of style, structure, depth, and content across all similar requests it has encountered.

Statistical averages are, by definition, specifically useful for no particular situation. They are the mean across all situations — which means they adequately serve the situation that exactly matches the mean, and inadequately serve every specific situation that differs from it. Most real operational needs differ from the mean. This is why unconstrained AI outputs so reliably feel generic.

Constraints solve this problem by reducing the probability space — not by limiting the model's intelligence, but by directing it. A well-designed constraint eliminates irrelevant regions of the probability space and concentrates the model's generative capacity on the relevant ones. The model is not less capable under constraint. It is more precisely capable — its full analytical capacity applied to the actual target rather than spread across the statistical average of all possible targets.

5.1 Constraint Failure Analysis: Learning from What Goes Wrong

Before understanding optimal constraint architecture, it is essential to understand constraint failure modes — the specific ways in which poor constraint design degrades output quality. Each failure mode has a distinct signature that allows diagnosis and correction.

```
FAILURE MODE 1: TOO FEW CONSTRAINTS
Prompt: 'Write a market analysis for our
technology product.'
Result: Generic overview covering competitive
landscape, customer segments, pricing,
distribution, and trends - all at identical,
shallow depth. No prioritization. Could apply to
any technology product in any market in any year.
Mechanism: Maximum interpretive spread. Model
selected statistical average across all market
analysis requests.
Diagnosis: Objective is present but unqualified.
The model knows what to produce (a market
analysis) but has no guidance on which dimensions
matter, which segment is relevant, what decision
the analysis is intended to support, or what
depth is appropriate.

FAILURE MODE 2: TOO MANY CONSTRAINTS
Prompt: 'Write a market analysis. Be
comprehensive. Be concise. Cover all segments.
Focus on enterprise only. Use formal language. Be
accessible to non-experts. Prioritize data. Avoid
jargon. Be specific. Be strategic. Include
tactical details.'
Result: Incoherent. Contradictory instructions
fragment the output. Formal language conflicts
```

with accessible framing. Comprehensive coverage conflicts with conciseness. Segment instructions conflict with each other.

Mechanism: Constraint overload. Competing directives create a contradictory probability space that the model cannot resolve coherently.

Diagnosis: More constraints do not automatically produce more alignment. Constraints must be coherent and non-conflicting. The number of constraints should reflect the actual complexity of the specification, not the operator's desire to be thorough.

FAILURE MODE 3: CONFLICTING CONSTRAINTS

Prompt: 'Analyze risks comprehensively. Keep it brief. Be specific about mechanisms. Maintain a high-level executive view.'

Result: Internally inconsistent. Comprehensive risk analysis conflicts with briefness. Mechanistic specificity conflicts with executive high-level framing.

Mechanism: Logical constraint conflict. The constraints cannot be simultaneously satisfied – any output that fully satisfies one partially violates another.

Diagnosis: Constraint architecture requires internal consistency. Before applying multiple constraints, verify that they can be simultaneously satisfied. Where genuine tension exists, establish explicit priority hierarchy.

FAILURE MODE 4: MISPLACED CONSTRAINT HIERARCHY

Prompt: 'PRIMARY PRIORITY: Speed of analysis. SECONDARY PRIORITY: Accuracy. TERTIARY PRIORITY: Thoroughness.'

Result: Fast, shallow, potentially inaccurate output – which is exactly what was specified, but not what the operator actually wanted.

Mechanism: The hierarchy was stated but incorrectly ordered for the actual goal.

Diagnosis: Constraint hierarchy must reflect actual priorities, not stated priorities. The operator who writes 'primary: speed' and is disappointed by shallow output has miscommunicated their actual priority ordering.

Each failure mode is correctable through specific architectural adjustments. The operator who learns to recognize failure mode signatures can diagnose prompt architecture problems quickly and apply targeted corrections rather than making unfocused revisions.

5.2 The Constraint Design Matrix

Natural CodeLex organizes constraints into seven operational categories, each targeting a distinct dimension of generation behavior. Understanding these categories allows operators to design comprehensive constraint architecture that addresses all relevant behavioral dimensions simultaneously.

> SCOPE CONSTRAINTS — What the model should focus on
>
> Function: Reduces irrelevant expansion by defining the analytical territory explicitly.
>
> Example: 'Analyze operational inefficiencies only. Exclude marketing strategy, compensation structure, and product features.'
>
> When to use: When outputs consistently drift into adjacent topics. When the model is covering too many variables at shallow depth instead of fewer variables at appropriate depth.
>
> IDENTITY CONSTRAINTS — What professional perspective should dominate
>
> Function: Activates domain-specific language patterns, analytical frameworks, and epistemic standards.
>
> Example: 'Operate as a senior forensic auditor. Apply conservative evidentiary standards. Treat absence of documentation as a risk indicator, not as confirmation of absence of risk.'
>
> When to use: When outputs lack domain-specific depth. When the model is producing generalist analysis of a specialist problem.
>
> TONE CONSTRAINTS — What stylistic behavior should characterize the output
>
> Function: Stabilizes voice consistency and prevents stylistic drift.
>
> Example: 'Direct executive language throughout. No hedging qualifiers. No softening language. If uncertain, flag explicitly rather than using vague phrasing to mask uncertainty.'
>
> When to use: When outputs drift stylistically across a session. When the model is adding

diplomatic softening that undermines analytical clarity.

SOURCE CONSTRAINTS — What informational boundaries apply

Function: Reduces hallucination risk by anchoring the model to verified material.

Example: 'Use only the three documents provided. Do not introduce outside information. If a relevant consideration is not addressed in the provided material, note the gap rather than filling it with general knowledge.'

When to use: When outputs contain information that cannot be traced to provided material. When factual accuracy is critical and the model's training data is potentially unreliable for the specific topic.

LOGIC CONSTRAINTS — What reasoning requirements must be met

Function: Improves analytical integrity by specifying how conclusions must be reached.

Example: 'Reach conclusions only from documented evidence in the provided material. Distinguish between direct evidence, reasonable inference, and speculative assessment. Flag each category explicitly.'

When to use: When outputs contain confident assertions that appear to be inferences presented as facts. When the decision stakes require high analytical rigor.

FORMATTING CONSTRAINTS — What structural requirements the output must meet

Function: Improves usability and consistency. Gives the model a target shape to generate toward.

Example: 'Output format: Risk matrix with four columns — Risk Description, Regulatory Basis (cite specific provision), Severity (Critical/High/Medium/Low), Recommended Action. Maximum ten rows.'

When to use: For outputs that will be used in specific downstream contexts requiring specific formats. When consistency across multiple sessions matters.

VERIFICATION CONSTRAINTS — What quality standards must be met

```
Function: Embeds epistemological accountability
into the output rather than leaving quality
assessment to post-generation review.
Example: 'Assign confidence levels
(High/Medium/Low) to each finding. Flag any
finding that depends on an assumption not
validated by the provided material. Note if any
source material directly contradicts a finding.'
When to use: For analytical outputs that will
inform consequential decisions. When the operator
needs to assess output reliability without
independent domain expertise.
```

The full power of the Constraint Design Matrix comes from combining multiple categories simultaneously. A prompt that addresses scope, identity, source, and verification simultaneously creates a far more stable operational environment than one that addresses only scope. Each category eliminates a different dimension of interpretive uncertainty, and their combined effect is multiplicative rather than merely additive.

5.3 Negative Prompting

Among the constraint techniques available to AI operators, negative prompting — explicitly defining what should be excluded — is among the most powerful and the most consistently underused.

Most operators focus on positive specification: telling the model what to do, what to include, what to prioritize. This is necessary but incomplete. Language models have strong default tendencies — patterns of generation that are statistically most common in their training data and therefore most likely to appear in the absence of other instructions. These defaults are often the exact patterns that produce generic, low-value outputs.

Negative constraints directly suppress these defaults. They are not redundant with positive constraints — they address different aspects of the probability distribution. A positive constraint narrows the model toward the target. A negative constraint eliminates the specific default patterns that are most likely to contaminate the output.

The most valuable negative constraints for common enterprise tasks:

```
FOR EXECUTIVE COMMUNICATION:
- No motivational language ('exciting
opportunity,' 'great momentum,' 'positive
trajectory')
- No generic introductions ('In today's fast-
paced environment...' / 'As we navigate
unprecedented change...')
- No passive voice constructions when active
voice is available
- No marketing adjectives (innovative,
transformative, disruptive, cutting-edge)
- No hedge-softening that obscures clear
positions ('it may be worth considering
whether...')

FOR ANALYTICAL WRITING:
- No summary paragraphs that repeat what was just
stated
- No transitional elaboration ('Building on the
above analysis...' / 'As we have seen...')
- No academic hedging when confident conclusions
are warranted
- No scope-expanding qualifications that broaden
the analysis beyond the specified focus
- No prescriptive recommendations when diagnosis-
only was specified

FOR TECHNICAL DOCUMENTATION:
- No introductory context that restates what the
reader already knows
- No conceptual elaboration on established
principles
- No comparative framing that references
alternatives not under consideration
- No uncertainty language where the technical
answer is definitive
```

Negative prompting is particularly valuable because it targets probabilistic defaults — the patterns that are most deeply embedded in training distributions and therefore most likely to appear in the absence of explicit suppression. A negative constraint that eliminates the top three default patterns for a given task type can produce more improvement in output quality than any equivalent positive constraint, because it removes the specific interference patterns most likely to degrade the signal.

5.4 Constraint Tradeoffs: Navigating Real Tensions

Constraint design is not a matter of applying maximum constraint everywhere. Different tasks, different workflow phases, and different quality requirements call for different constraint profiles — and advanced operators navigate these tradeoffs deliberately.

```
CREATIVITY vs. PRECISION
The tension: Tight constraints improve analytical
precision but can prevent the model from
surfacing unexpected connections or generating
genuinely novel approaches. Maximum precision
constraints produce reliable outputs within
defined territory – but they may prevent the
model from reaching outside that territory to
find insights that the operator did not know to
look for.

Navigation: Apply exploratory constraints in
early ideation phases (broad scope, minimal
exclusions, generative identity) and precision
constraints in later analytical or delivery
phases (narrow scope, explicit exclusions,
specialist identity). The workflow should move
from exploratory to constrained, not remain
constant throughout.

EXPLORATION vs. STABILITY
The tension: Open-ended early phases allow
broader ideation and may surface valuable
directions the operator had not considered.
Stability constraints prevent this exploration
but produce more reliable, consistent outputs
that can be systematically refined.

Navigation: Phase the constraint profile. Use
minimal constraints in discovery phases to allow
the model to surface the full possibility space.
Add stabilizing constraints progressively as the
analytical direction crystallizes. The final
synthesis phase should operate under the tightest
constraint architecture.
```

```
FLEXIBILITY vs. RELIABILITY
The tension: Highly specific formatting and
structural constraints improve output consistency
and replicability but reduce the model's ability
to adapt its output structure to what the content
actually requires.

Navigation: Apply strict formatting constraints
for outputs with specific downstream use
requirements (reports that will be directly used,
communications that will be sent, analyses that
must be compared across sessions). Apply flexible
formatting for exploratory analysis where the
output will be reviewed and revised before use.

DEPTH vs. BREADTH
The tension: Narrow scope constraints produce
deep analysis of specific topics at the cost of
adjacent considerations. Broad scope allows
comprehensive coverage at the cost of depth
within any single area.

Navigation: Resolve through explicit
prioritization rather than through vague
instructions. 'Prioritize depth on operational
risk factors, breadth on market factors' is a
more useful instruction than 'be comprehensive.'
When both depth and breadth are required,
decompose the task into sequential phases rather
than attempting to satisfy both simultaneously.
```

5.5 Constraint Weighting and Hierarchy

Not all constraints carry equal weight in shaping model behavior. Some instructions strongly dominate generation behavior; others fade into background noise, particularly in longer sessions where attentional competition increases.

Several factors affect constraint weight. Position matters — constraints established early in a prompt typically receive higher salience than those buried in the middle. Explicit labeling matters — constraints marked as PRIMARY or CRITICAL receive more attentional weight than unlabeled ones. Structural formatting matters — constraints presented in prominent formatting receive more weight than those embedded in prose. Repetition within reason matters — a constraint reinforced once mid-session maintains influence better than one stated only at the start.

For critical constraints — those whose violation would make the output unusable — explicit priority marking is essential:

```
CRITICAL CONSTRAINT – NON-NEGOTIABLE:
Source-bound reasoning only. If a finding cannot
be directly supported by text in the provided
documents, it must not appear in the output. This
constraint takes priority over comprehensiveness,
analytical elegance, and flow. A shorter, source-
bound output is always preferable to a longer
output that includes unsupported claims.
```

This level of explicit priority marking creates a strong attentional signal that the model processes differently from ordinary instructions. It signals that this constraint is structurally dominant — that it should not be traded off against other objectives even when such trades would produce more complete-seeming outputs.

5.6 Constraint Decay and Reinforcement

One of the most important and least visible aspects of constraint management is decay — the gradual weakening of constraint influence over the course of a long session as new context enters the window and earlier instructions lose attentional salience.

Constraint decay is not dramatic or sudden. It is gradual and cumulative. A constraint that strongly shapes output in the first three exchanges may have half its influence by exchange ten and a quarter of its influence by exchange twenty, simply because each new exchange adds content that competes for the same attentional resources that the constraint requires to remain influential.

This phenomenon explains a common frustration: the AI 'stops listening' to instructions as a session progresses. The model has not stopped listening. The constraint has lost attentional competition to the accumulated context. The solution is periodic reinforcement — not because the model needs to be reminded, but because reinforcement re-establishes the constraint's attentional salience in the current context window:

```
MID-SESSION REINFORCEMENT BLOCK:

Reinforcing operating constraints for this
session:
- Source-bound reasoning only – no outside
information
- Forensic audit identity – conservative
evidentiary standards
- Risk-ranked output format
- Flag all speculative inferences explicitly

These constraints remain in effect for all
subsequent analysis in this session.
```

Reinforcement blocks cost relatively few tokens and produce significant alignment benefits in long sessions. The operator who reinforces constraints at regular intervals — every ten to fifteen exchanges in complex sessions — will consistently produce better outputs in the second half of a session than the operator who relies solely on initial constraint establishment.

Final Principle: Constraints as Alignment Architecture

Constraints are not limitations on AI capability. They are mechanisms for alignment — tools that direct the model's generative capacity toward the actual target rather than distributing it across the statistical average of all possible targets.

Weak constraints produce drift, ambiguity, hallucination risk, and outputs that feel generically correct but specifically useless. Strong constraints — coherent, appropriately weighted, actively maintained, and deliberately designed across all seven constraint dimensions — produce focus, precision, analytical clarity, and operational reliability.

The paradox at the center of constraint design is that boundaries are not the enemy of capability. They are its architecture. The model's intelligence is not diminished by well-designed constraints. It is directed — concentrated on the actual problem rather than spread across the statistical average of all problems that superficially resemble it.

Advanced prompting is not about saying more. It is about shaping probability with precision. And constraints, properly designed, are the most powerful instruments available for doing exactly that.

CHAPTER 6

THE FRACTURE OF IDENTITY

Role Simulation, Archetypes, and Behavioral Framing

Ask an AI system to act as a forensic auditor, and something changes. The vocabulary shifts. The risk thresholds recalibrate. The analytical emphasis moves toward evidence standards and liability exposure. The tone becomes more conservative, more precise, more likely to flag uncertainty than paper over it.

Ask the same system to act as a startup growth strategist, and different patterns emerge. The same problems that the auditor treated as risks become opportunities in the strategist's framing. Speed replaces caution. Market upside replaces downside protection. The analytical posture transforms.

Neither output is intrinsically superior. Each is appropriate for different decisions, different contexts, and different organizational needs. The fact that the same underlying system can produce both — and that the operator can direct which one appears — is one of the most powerful and most misunderstood capabilities in AI prompting.

Natural CodeLex calls this capability Identity Framing: the structured use of professional role assignment to activate domain-specific language patterns, analytical priorities, and behavioral orientations that make AI outputs more appropriate for specific contexts. Understanding both the power and the limits of identity framing is essential for operators who want to use it reliably rather than occasionally.

6.1 The Mechanism: Probability Weighting, Not Transformation

Before examining what identity framing can do, it is essential to understand what it actually is — because the misconception is both common and operationally consequential.

Identity framing does not transform the model into a different system. It does not give the model genuine professional expertise that it lacked before the identity instruction. It does not create anything resembling the lived experience, professional accountability, or deep contextual judgment that human professionals develop through years of consequential practice.

What identity framing does is alter the probability weighting of the generation process — activating statistical patterns in the model's training data that are associated with the specified identity. When a model is instructed to operate as a forensic auditor, it begins generating language that is statistically characteristic of forensic auditing contexts: conservative evidentiary language, risk-escalating framing, procedural precision, formal documentation standards. Not because the model has become an auditor, but because these patterns are highly associated in training data with the concept of forensic auditing.

This distinction matters practically. Probability weighting can produce outputs that are dramatically more appropriate for specific contexts than unframed outputs — which is genuinely valuable. But it does not produce outputs that should be treated as equivalent to actual professional judgment. The forensic auditor identity produces forensic-auditor-flavored analysis. It does not produce forensic audit results that can substitute for the work of an actual forensic auditor.

Advanced operators hold both of these truths simultaneously: identity framing is a powerful productivity tool that substantially improves output quality for domain-specific tasks, and it is a simulation of professional language patterns rather than a replication of professional expertise.

6.2 The ELIZA Effect and the Psychology of Anthropomorphism

The psychological tendency to attribute genuine understanding and expertise to AI systems that simulate professional language is one of the most significant cognitive risks in AI usage — and it becomes more pronounced, not less, as AI systems become more capable.

As introduced in Chapter 1, Joseph Weizenbaum's 1966 ELIZA experiment at MIT is the defining demonstration of this effect. ELIZA was a pattern-matching program that simulated a psychotherapist by reflecting users' statements back as questions — no genuine understanding of language, no reasoning capacity, no model of human psychology whatsoever. Yet users — including highly educated professionals explicitly told it was a program — consistently attributed understanding, empathy, and genuine therapeutic insight to it. Some refused to continue using it once they understood what it was. Weizenbaum was so disturbed by his users' responses that he spent the rest of his career writing about the dangers of anthropomorphizing computers.

The ELIZA effect — the systematic human tendency to attribute mental states, understanding, and genuine expertise to systems producing coherent language — has only intensified as AI systems have become more sophisticated. When a model maintains professional vocabulary, applies analytical frameworks coherently, produces structurally sophisticated output, and does so across an extended conversation, the psychological experience of interacting with expertise is genuine and powerful — even when the operator knows, intellectually, that the underlying mechanism is statistical pattern generation.

This creates a specific and important risk in identity framing contexts. Operators who instruct a model to act as a legal expert, medical professional, or financial advisor may receive outputs that feel authoritative, comprehensive, and professionally credible — and may grant those outputs a level of trust that the underlying generation mechanism does not warrant. The simulation of expertise is not expertise. The language of certainty is not certainty. The structure of professional analysis is not professional analysis.

Advanced operators maintain what might be called calibrated skepticism — a sustained awareness that the psychological experience of interacting with expertise and the actual quality of the underlying analysis are related but not identical. They use identity-framed outputs as starting points for expert review, as scaffolding for their own analytical development, and as productivity amplifiers for work that will be validated through other means. They do not treat them as substitutes for the actual expertise they simulate.

6.3 Multi-Identity Demonstration: The Same Problem Through Four Lenses

One of the most powerful illustrations of identity framing's operational value is running the same business problem through multiple professional identities simultaneously — revealing the different risk profiles, analytical emphases, and strategic considerations that different professional perspectives surface.

The following demonstrates this with a specific enterprise decision:

```
SCENARIO: A 300-person professional services firm
is evaluating acquiring a 50-person boutique
competitor at a $15M valuation. The target has
strong client relationships but aging technology
infrastructure and three key senior employees
whose retention post-acquisition is uncertain.

LEGAL IDENTITY ANALYSIS (Senior M&A counsel)


Primary analytical emphasis: Liability exposure,
contractual obligations, IP ownership, employment
law, regulatory compliance.


Key findings that would be prioritized:
- Client contract transferability: Do client
agreements contain change-of-control provisions
that would allow clients to exit post-
acquisition? Percentage of revenue at risk?
```

- Employee agreements: Do key employee retention packages create contractual obligations? What are the non-compete and non-solicitation provisions for departing employees?
- Technology IP ownership: Is the aging infrastructure owned outright or subject to third-party licensing agreements with change-of-control triggers?
- Representations and warranties: What indemnification structures are appropriate given the technology liability exposure?
- Regulatory considerations: Are there professional licensing or regulatory approvals required for the acquisition in relevant practice areas?

Characteristic language: 'creates material exposure,' 'requires representation,' 'subject to indemnification,' 'prior to execution,' 'documented evidence required.'

CFO IDENTITY ANALYSIS (Chief Financial Officer)

Primary analytical emphasis: Valuation accuracy, integration cost, revenue synergies, cash flow impact, margin implications.

Key findings that would be prioritized:
- Valuation basis: Does the $15M valuation reflect client relationship value (relationship-dependent, therefore risky) or recurring revenue value (more reliable)? What is the implied EBITDA multiple?
- Integration cost modeling: Technology infrastructure replacement will require capital investment. The financial model must include full integration costs, not just acquisition price.
- Revenue retention risk: Key employee uncertainty creates client retention uncertainty. Scenario analysis on 10%, 25%, and 40% client revenue loss post-acquisition is required before valuation can be validated.
- Synergy timeline: Revenue synergies in professional services acquisitions typically take 18–36 months to materialize. Cash flow implications in the interim period require modeling.
- Earnout structure: Key employee retention and client retention risk suggests earnout provisions contingent on both.

Characteristic language: 'EBITDA multiple,' 'scenario analysis,' 'NPV of synergies,' 'integration cost assumptions,' 'earnout structure.'

HR/PEOPLE IDENTITY ANALYSIS (Chief People Officer)

Primary analytical emphasis: Cultural compatibility, talent retention, organizational integration, leadership dynamics.

Key findings that would be prioritized:

- Three key employee retention: What is known about their motivations? Are they likely motivated by autonomy (a boutique value proposition often eroded by acquisition), financial upside (address through equity), or mission alignment (requires cultural due diligence)?
- Cultural compatibility: Professional services acquisitions frequently fail due to cultural incompatibility. What is the target firm's leadership style relative to the acquirer? Are billing practices, work-life expectations, and professional development philosophies compatible?
- Integration timeline: Rushed integration typically destroys the value that made the acquisition attractive. What is the minimum viable integration timeline that preserves client relationship continuity?
- Organizational redundancy: Which functions overlap, and what are the retention versus elimination decisions? What severance obligations and morale impacts result from those decisions?

Characteristic language: 'retention risk,' 'cultural due diligence,' 'integration timeline,' 'employee value proposition,' 'organizational design.'

CRITICAL INSIGHT UNIQUE TO THIS IDENTITY: The three key employees are likely considering the acquisition primarily as a threat to the autonomy and culture that made the boutique attractive to them. Financial retention packages alone may be insufficient. A defined operational independence commitment for a transition period may be more effective.

```
TECHNOLOGY IDENTITY ANALYSIS (Chief Technology
Officer)

Primary analytical emphasis: Technical debt,
infrastructure compatibility, systems
integration, security posture.

Key findings that would be prioritized:
- Technology infrastructure assessment: 'Aging
infrastructure' requires specific definition. Is
it operationally unreliable, technically
obsolete, or simply visually dated? The
remediation cost and timeline differ dramatically
across these scenarios.
- Integration complexity: Can the target's
systems integrate with the acquirer's existing
infrastructure, or does acquisition require
parallel operation of incompatible systems during
a migration period?
- Data migration risk: Client data migration is a
significant operational risk in professional
services acquisitions. What are the data
architecture differences, and what migration
timeline is realistic?
- Security posture: Cybersecurity due diligence
is non-negotiable. Client data liability exposure
from an inherited security breach could exceed
the acquisition value.
- Hidden infrastructure costs: The technology
infrastructure replacement cost is likely not
fully reflected in the $15M valuation. An
independent technical assessment is required
before price validation.

CRITICAL INSIGHT UNIQUE TO THIS IDENTITY: The
financial model likely underestimates technology
integration costs by 40-60%. The legal and
financial analyses treat technology risk as a
qualifier. It may be an acquisition-blocking
issue depending on assessment findings.
```

Four professional identities. One acquisition decision. Four substantially different risk profiles — each surfacing considerations that the others would minimize or miss entirely. The legal identity surfaces client contract transferability risk that neither the financial nor technology analyses would prioritize. The technology identity surfaces infrastructure cost underestimation that invalidates the financial model. The people identity surfaces the insight that financial retention alone may be insufficient — an insight that neither legal nor financial framing is positioned to generate.

The value of multi-identity analysis is not that any one identity is more correct than the others. It is that the full risk topology of a complex decision only becomes visible when multiple professional perspectives are applied systematically rather than relying on a single analytical lens.

6.4 Weak vs. Strong Identity Framing

The difference between identity framing that produces meaningfully different outputs and identity framing that produces superficial stylistic variation lies entirely in the specificity and depth of the identity specification.

Weak identity framing generates weak behavioral differentiation because it fails to activate the specific pattern clusters that make professional perspectives operationally distinct. Strong identity framing activates those clusters by providing sufficient specificity to narrow the probability space toward the characteristic patterns of the specified role.

```
WEAK IDENTITY FRAMING:
'Act like an expert.'

Problem: Expert in what domain? At what
organizational level? With what analytical
philosophy? What risk orientation? What
evidentiary standards? What communication style?
The instruction is too broad to activate
meaningful behavioral differentiation. The model
has no guidance on which expert pattern cluster
to activate.

Result: Marginally more confident-sounding output
with minimal analytical differentiation.

STRONG IDENTITY FRAMING:
IDENTITY: Senior enterprise risk auditor with 15+
years specializing in operational compliance for
regulated financial services institutions.
```

```
ANALYTICAL PHILOSOPHY: Treat absence of
documentation as risk, not as absence of risk.
Prioritize findings with regulatory exposure over
theoretical risks with no enforcement history.

COMMUNICATION STYLE: Direct, formal, evidence-
cited. No diplomatic softening of material
findings. Uncertainty should be flagged
explicitly rather than masked by hedge language.

EVIDENTIARY STANDARDS: Conservative. Source every
material claim. Distinguish between findings
supported by direct documentation, reasonable
inference, and speculative assessment.

Result: Substantially different analytical
posture, vocabulary, risk prioritization, and
evidentiary standards — because the identity
specification is detailed enough to activate a
specific and coherent pattern cluster.
```

The additional specificity in the strong framing is not merely decorative. Each element activates a different aspect of the target professional pattern cluster. The analytical philosophy instruction shifts the model's default stance from risk-neutral to risk-conservative. The communication style instruction suppresses the diplomatic softening default. The evidentiary standards instruction activates the source-citation and confidence-flagging patterns associated with auditing contexts. Together, they produce a behavioral profile that is meaningfully distinct from a generalist analytical response.

6.5 Identity Drift and Contamination

Identity framing, like all contextual structures, is subject to decay and contamination over extended sessions. Understanding these failure modes allows operators to design against them proactively.

IDENTITY DRIFT is the gradual weakening of a simulated professional role as the session accumulates contextual residue from incompatible exchanges. A forensic audit identity established at the beginning of a session will drift toward more conversational, less technically precise patterns if the session includes casual exchanges, emotional discussions, or brainstorming interludes. The drift is subtle and cumulative — individual exchanges may not appear to cause significant degradation, but the accumulated effect across many exchanges can substantially alter the behavioral profile.

IDENTITY CONTAMINATION is a more acute failure mode in which the residue from a specific incompatible contextual block actively pollutes the simulated identity. An operator who spends thirty exchanges developing motivational communication with a warm, collaborative, emotionally empathetic framing, and then requests forensic compliance analysis from the same session, will often receive analysis that carries the warmth and collaborative framing forward — producing output that is too narratively accessible, too diplomatically hedged, and too focused on stakeholder relationships to function as genuine forensic analysis.

Both failure modes require similar interventions. The most effective response is explicit re-grounding — a structured instruction that resets the identity frame with sufficient specificity to overcome the accumulated drift:

```
IDENTITY RESET INSTRUCTION:

[IDENTITY RESET]

Disregard tonal and stylistic patterns from
previous conversation. The warm, collaborative
framing appropriate for stakeholder communication
is not appropriate for this task.

RE-ESTABLISHING IDENTITY: Senior forensic
compliance auditor.

BEHAVIORAL RESET:
- Conservative evidentiary standards
- No narrative elaboration — findings only
- Direct language — no diplomatic softening
- Source every material claim
- Flag uncertainty explicitly rather than using
hedge language
```

```
This identity remains in effect for all
subsequent analysis in this session.

[RESET COMPLETE]
```

The explicit reset instruction, combined with the re-specification of key behavioral elements, typically produces a substantial behavioral correction even within a contaminated session. The more detailed the re-specification, the more complete the recovery.

6.6 Identity Collision and Hierarchy

Advanced workflows sometimes require multiple professional identities to operate within the same analysis — either sequentially (the same problem analyzed through different lenses in succession) or simultaneously (a multi-perspective evaluation that must integrate competing viewpoints into a unified recommendation). When multiple identities are present, collision risk — the blending of incompatible behavioral patterns into an incoherent amalgam — requires active management through explicit identity hierarchy.

The acquisition scenario demonstrates this clearly. A legal identity and a growth strategist identity have fundamentally incompatible orientations: one defaults toward risk escalation, conservative evidentiary standards, and caution; the other defaults toward opportunity identification, tolerance for uncertainty, and speed. Without explicit hierarchy, the model will blend these patterns in ways that serve neither — producing analysis that is insufficiently cautious for legal purposes and insufficiently ambitious for strategic ones.

Identity hierarchy addresses this by designating a primary identity that governs the synthesis and final output, with secondary identities contributing constrained input:

```
MULTI-IDENTITY HIERARCHY STRUCTURE:
```

```
PRIMARY IDENTITY: Legal compliance perspective —
governs final conclusions and risk assessment.

SECONDARY IDENTITY: Strategic growth perspective
— contributes opportunity analysis as input only.
Not to override compliance conclusions.

INTEGRATION INSTRUCTION: Where compliance and
strategic perspectives conflict, present the
conflict explicitly. Do not resolve conflicts
through compromise language that obscures the
genuine tension. The decision about how to
resolve the conflict belongs to the human
reviewer, not the analysis.

OUTPUT STRUCTURE: Compliance assessment first.
Strategic considerations second. Explicit
conflict identification third. No artificial
reconciliation.
```

This hierarchy structure prevents identity collision while preserving the value of both perspectives. The legal identity governs the output's epistemic standards and risk characterization. The strategic identity contributes opportunity analysis that the legal identity would minimize. The explicit conflict identification preserves the genuine tension rather than resolving it artificially — which is exactly what allows a human decision-maker to make an informed choice.

6.7 Synthetic Expertise vs. Real Expertise: The Critical Distinction

The principle that identity framing is probability weighting rather than genuine expertise creation has direct operational implications that must be stated clearly and unambiguously.

AI identity framing should function as a productivity amplifier and analytical scaffold for work that will be validated through appropriate expert review. It should not function as a substitute for that review in contexts where the quality and reliability of the analysis is consequential.

The forensic auditor identity produces forensic-auditor-flavored analysis. The patterns it activates are associated with forensic auditing in training data — which means they reflect the vocabulary, analytical frameworks, and epistemic standards typical of forensic auditing contexts. But training data associations are not professional expertise. A forensic auditor brings decades of pattern recognition from actual audits, accountability for the professional validity of their conclusions, awareness of jurisdiction-specific regulatory nuance, and judgment calibrated through exposure to the consequences of errors. None of these are present in identity-framed AI outputs.

This matters practically because identity-framed outputs can be remarkably good at producing the surface features of expert analysis — the vocabulary, the structure, the apparent thoroughness — while containing analytical errors that would be immediately visible to a genuine domain expert. The appearance of expertise, produced fluently and consistently, creates exactly the conditions for the ELIZA effect to operate most dangerously: the output sounds like expert analysis, which makes it feel like expert analysis, which creates pressure to treat it as expert analysis.

The appropriate use model for identity framing in high-stakes domains: use it to accelerate the analytical scaffolding, to surface the right questions, to structure the right framework, and to produce a high-quality draft that a domain expert can review efficiently. Do not use it to replace the expert review itself.

Final Principle: Identity as Probability Architecture

Identity framing is one of the most powerful tools in the advanced operator's toolkit — not because it creates genuine expertise, but because it reliably activates the specific pattern clusters that make AI outputs more appropriate for specific analytical contexts.

Used well, it transforms generic AI outputs into domain-specific analysis that reflects the characteristic vocabulary, analytical priorities, risk orientations, and epistemic standards of the specified professional role. Used poorly — with vague identity specifications, without awareness of drift and contamination, without understanding of the simulation vs. expertise distinction — it produces superficial stylistic variation that does not justify the complexity it adds.

The model responds not only to instructions. It responds to perspective. And perspective — defined precisely, maintained actively, and applied with clear understanding of its nature and limits — shapes probability in ways that produce substantially more useful outputs than any amount of prompt revision without it.

CHAPTER 7

THE ECONOMICS OF ATTENTION

Token Pressure, Signal Density, and the Architecture of Cognitive Compression

There is a wall every serious AI operator eventually hits.

It arrives without warning. A session that has been producing strong, focused output suddenly slows. Responses become generic. Earlier constraints stop holding. The model begins blending objectives that were cleanly separated an hour ago. Then the system returns an error, or simply truncates — the context window has reached its limit.

Most operators interpret this as a technical inconvenience. A ceiling imposed by the platform. Something to work around by starting a new chat.

Advanced operators interpret it differently. They recognize the context limit not as a ceiling but as a mirror — a precise reflection of how efficiently they have been using the available cognitive space. Operators who hit the limit early are almost always carrying enormous amounts of contextual waste: redundant instructions, emotional padding, re-explained objectives, accumulated conversational noise that consumes tokens without improving output quality.

The token limit is partly a platform constraint. It is also a workflow discipline problem.

This chapter addresses both dimensions — the structural reality of finite AI attention, and the practical strategies that allow operators to work effectively within it, extend it intelligently, and design workflows that never burn tokens on waste.

7.1 Attention Is Not Infinite

Most users interact with AI systems as though they are limitless conversational spaces — capable of processing everything equally, retaining every detail perfectly, and maintaining precision regardless of how much context accumulates.

This is not how large language models behave.

Every AI session operates within a context window — a finite space measured in tokens, where one token represents roughly three to four characters of text. Everything in that window competes for the model's attention simultaneously: your instructions, your documents, the conversation history, your constraints, your examples, your clarifications, and every correction you have typed since the session began.

Claude Shannon's information theory established in the 1940s that communication systems have finite capacity — and that signal competes directly with noise for that capacity. AI context windows operate under an identical constraint. Every token of noise displaces a token of signal. There is no neutral content. Everything either helps or hurts.

Natural CodeLex treats prompting not only as language design, but as resource allocation. The operator is constantly deciding — consciously or not — what deserves space in the context window and what does not.

7.2 What Tokens Actually Cost

Understanding token economics requires understanding what actually consumes context space. Most operators dramatically underestimate the token cost of their habits.

```
HIGH TOKEN COST BEHAVIORS:

Conversational preamble – 'That's a great point,
and I think what you're getting at is...' before
every substantive response burns tokens on social
lubrication that produces zero analytical value.

Repeated re-explanation – Restating the objective
at the beginning of each prompt because the
operator isn't confident the model remembers.
This compounds rapidly across a long session.
```

> Emotional qualification – 'I'm not sure if this is the right approach, but...' and similar hedging language consumes tokens while signaling uncertainty that actively degrades output confidence.
>
> Passive construction – 'It would be helpful if you could perhaps consider analyzing...' versus 'Analyze.' The verbose version uses eight times the tokens to communicate the same instruction.
>
> Unnecessary examples – Illustrating a pattern twice when once would suffice. Each additional example consumes tokens and can introduce interpretive noise if the examples subtly conflict.
>
> Accumulated history – Every previous exchange in a long session remains in the context window. A session that has covered five different topics carries the full weight of all five, whether they remain relevant or not.

The cumulative effect is significant. An operator who consistently uses verbose prompting, re-explains context, and runs multi-topic sessions in a single thread may be consuming two to three times more tokens per unit of useful work than an operator with disciplined session architecture.

7.3 The Attention Budget Framework

Natural CodeLex introduces the Attention Budget Framework: a way of thinking about prompt design as finite cognitive resource allocation.

> SALIENCE – How much influence does each element of the prompt actually exert on the model's generation process? High-salience elements dominate output behavior. Low-salience elements consume tokens without contributing alignment. Position matters: elements near the beginning and end of a prompt typically receive higher salience than those buried in the middle.
>
> ATTENTION COMPETITION – When two high-salience instructions conflict, the model attempts to

```
satisfy both simultaneously — producing output
that partially satisfies each while fully
satisfying neither. This is why constraint
conflicts are so operationally expensive: they
don't just fail to help, they actively fragment
the model's generative focus.

SIGNAL HIERARCHY — Well-structured prompts create
implicit importance rankings that the model
processes proportionally. Explicitly labeled
priorities (PRIMARY, SECONDARY, TERTIARY) create
clearer allocation signals than implied
hierarchy.

TOKEN PRESSURE — As context length increases,
earlier elements experience declining influence.
Instructions established at the beginning of a
long session gradually lose salience as new
content enters the window. This is why critical
constraints require periodic reinforcement in
extended workflows — not because the model
forgets, but because attentional competition
increases as the context fills.

COMPRESSION COST — Every summarization step
removes information. Compression that preserves
strategic priorities while eliminating noise
improves output quality. Compression that strips
nuance for the sake of brevity degrades
analytical integrity. The two must be
distinguished deliberately.
```

7.4 Structural Compression: The Techniques

The most direct response to token pressure is structural compression — redesigning prompt architecture to achieve maximum signal density with minimum token consumption.

```
USE LABELS INSTEAD OF SENTENCES

Verbose: 'I would like you to focus primarily on
identifying the key risks in this contract,
particularly around liability and indemnification
clauses.'

Compressed: 'OBJECTIVE: Extract liability and
indemnification risks.'
```

The compressed version communicates the same instruction in one fifth of the tokens. Multiplied across a complex session, this difference is substantial.

DROP ARTICLES AND TRANSITIONAL FILLER

Verbose: 'Please analyze the retention failures that we have been experiencing in the onboarding process.'

Compressed: 'Analyze onboarding retention failures.'

Eight tokens instead of twenty. The instruction is clearer, not less clear.

USE COLONS AND LINE BREAKS INSTEAD OF PROSE TRANSITIONS

Verbose: 'For the output, it would be most useful if you could provide a ranked list, and then for each item you could include a brief explanation of why it matters.'

Compressed:

OUTPUT:

- Ranked list
- Brief rationale per item

REPLACE PARAGRAPHS OF CONTEXT WITH BULLET HIERARCHIES

Verbose: 'We are a mid-sized financial services firm with about 200 employees, operating primarily in the southeastern United States. Our main compliance concern at the moment involves our data handling practices relative to the new regulatory requirements that came into effect this year.'

Compressed:

CONTEXT: 200-person financial services firm, SE United States.

PRIMARY CONCERN: Data handling compliance under current regulatory requirements.

These are not stylistic preferences. They are token engineering decisions that directly affect how much useful work a session can accomplish before hitting its limits.

7.5 Session Architecture: The Most Underused Tool

Structural compression at the prompt level addresses individual token waste. Session architecture addresses the larger pattern — how workflows are organized across sessions to preserve attention quality throughout.

Most operators who hit context limits frequently are not running sessions that are too long. They are running sessions that are too broad.

A single session covering strategic analysis, then document review, then communication drafting, then brainstorming, then back to strategic analysis accumulates contextual residue from all five domains simultaneously. The model carries the full weight of every topic shift. Signal from the strategic analysis competes with signal from the communication drafting competes with signal from the brainstorming.

The solution is session segmentation — treating each focused task as its own contained environment:

```
SINGLE-SESSION MISTAKE:
Session 1: Strategic analysis → document review →
communication drafting → brainstorming → back to
strategic analysis
Result: Context contamination, token waste,
degraded quality across all tasks.

SEGMENTED SESSION ARCHITECTURE:
Session 1: Strategic analysis only – with
compressed context stack, closed when complete.
Session 2: Document review only – fresh context,
identity-appropriate constraints, closed when
complete.
Session 3: Communication drafting only – clean
context, tone and format constraints established
upfront.
```

```
Each session uses its full context window for one
purpose. Quality is higher. Token efficiency is
dramatically better. The operator does more
useful work per token spent.
```

Starting a new session does not mean losing progress. It means carrying forward only what is actually relevant — which is almost always far less than operators assume.

7.6 The Compressed Handoff Block

The most powerful token-saving technique for operators working on complex multi-session projects is the Compressed Handoff Block — a dense summary of prior session findings that re-establishes context in a new session with minimum token cost.

Instead of pasting raw conversation history from a prior session (which can consume thousands of tokens of low-density content), the operator constructs a structured summary:

```
HANDOFF BLOCK TEMPLATE:

PROJECT: [Name/description – 1 line]

COMPLETED:
- [Key finding 1]
- [Key finding 2]
- [Key decision made]

ESTABLISHED CONSTRAINTS:
- [Constraint that must persist]
- [Constraint that must persist]

CURRENT SESSION OBJECTIVE: [Specific task for
this session only]

PRIOR CONTEXT TO IGNORE: [Topics from prior
sessions not relevant here]
```

A well-constructed Handoff Block re-establishes everything the new session needs in 100–200 tokens rather than the 2,000–5,000 tokens that raw conversation history would require. The new session begins with a clean context window, focused objective, and only the prior context that is operationally relevant.

This technique is particularly valuable for operators managing large, ongoing projects — strategy development, contract negotiations, research programs, organizational transformations — that extend across many sessions over days or weeks.

7.7 The Front-Loaded System Prompt

One of the highest-leverage session architecture techniques is the front-loaded system prompt — a single dense block at the beginning of a session that establishes everything the model needs to operate correctly, requiring minimal reinforcement throughout.

Most operators establish context gradually and conversationally — revealing objectives, constraints, and identity preferences through successive messages as they become relevant. This approach is inefficient. Each clarification consumes tokens and introduces the risk that earlier context has already influenced output before the correction arrives.

The front-loaded approach establishes the full operational environment before any substantive work begins:

```
FRONT-LOADED SYSTEM PROMPT STRUCTURE:

IDENTITY: [Professional role and domain]

SESSION OBJECTIVE: [What this session must
accomplish]

OPERATING CONSTRAINTS:
- [Critical constraint 1]
- [Critical constraint 2]
- [Critical constraint 3]

OUTPUT FORMAT: [What success looks like]
```

```
EXCLUSIONS: [What to ignore or avoid]

VERIFICATION STANDARD: [How claims should be
supported]

---
Begin.
```

A well-constructed front-loaded prompt costs 150–300 tokens upfront and eliminates the need for most mid-session corrections and clarifications. The net token economy is strongly positive — the upfront investment pays back across the entire session.

7.8 Shorthand and Semantic Compression

As operators develop recurring workflows, they can compress entire operational frameworks into shorthand references — dramatically reducing the token cost of re-establishing complex contexts.

```
An operator who regularly runs compliance
analysis might define at the beginning of a
session:

[CA] = Senior compliance auditor identity +
source-bound reasoning only + risk-ranked output
+ no speculation + regulatory exposure priority

Subsequent instructions can then invoke this
framework with two tokens rather than forty:
Analyze this contract as [CA].

Similarly:
[EB] = Executive briefing format: maximum 300
words, no jargon, decision-ready, ranked findings
only
[AR] = Adversarial review: challenge all
conclusions, identify unsupported assumptions,
surface alternative interpretations
```

Shorthand systems improve speed, consistency, and token efficiency simultaneously. However, they require stable underlying definitions — if the shorthand reference is ambiguous or inconsistently understood, it amplifies rather than resolves the problem. Shorthand that works well in one session context may behave differently in another if the surrounding context has shifted.

7.9 Before and After: Compression in Practice

The following examples demonstrate the full difference between verbose and compressed prompt architecture across three common enterprise tasks:

```
EXAMPLE 1 — CUSTOMER RETENTION ANALYSIS

VERBOSE (high noise):
'I'm looking for some ideas that might be helpful
in improving customer retention because we've
been having some issues lately with people not
staying long-term after they complete the
onboarding process. It would be great if you
could think about this from a few different
angles and maybe give us some suggestions about
what we might be able to do differently.'
Token cost: ~70 tokens. Interpretive spread: very
high.

COMPRESSED (high density):
OBJECTIVE: Identify onboarding failures reducing
90-day retention.
OUTPUT: Ranked bottlenecks with root cause
analysis.
EXCLUDE: Compensation analysis, product pricing.
Token cost: ~20 tokens. Interpretive spread:
narrow.

EXAMPLE 2 — LEGAL RISK REVIEW

VERBOSE (high noise):
'I need you to look at this contract and tell me
if there are any problems with it. I'm not a
lawyer so I might be missing some things. Just go
through it and tell me what you think might be
risky or could cause problems for us later on.'
Token cost: ~55 tokens. No identity, no source
constraint, no output specification.

COMPRESSED (high density):
IDENTITY: Senior M&A counsel.
```

```
TASK: Extract liability exposure and contractual
asymmetries.
SOURCE: Provided document only – no outside
assumptions.
OUTPUT: Ranked risk matrix, probability and
impact per item.
VERIFICATION: Flag all speculative inferences.
Token cost: ~35 tokens. Identity active, source-
bound, output specified, verification built in.

EXAMPLE 3 – EXECUTIVE BRIEFING

VERBOSE (high noise):
'Could you help me put together something for the
executive team that summarizes what's been
happening with the supply chain situation?
They'll want to know the key issues and probably
what we're planning to do about it. Try to keep
it professional and not too long.'
Token cost: ~60 tokens. Vague format, no length
constraint, no tone specification.

COMPRESSED (high density):
OBJECTIVE: Executive briefing on supply chain
disruption status.
FORMAT: Maximum 250 words. Three sections:
Situation / Key Risks / Next Actions.
TONE: Direct. No hedging language. No
motivational framing.
AUDIENCE: C-suite. Assume full operational
context.
Token cost: ~35 tokens. Format, length, tone,
audience – all established in one block.
```

7.10 Attention Saturation: The Enterprise Failure Mode

Inside enterprise environments, the most common token waste failure is Attention Saturation — sessions where too much material has been uploaded without task segmentation, forcing the model to distribute attention across an overwhelming volume of competing inputs.

The typical scenario: a senior leader uploads multiple reports, contracts, strategic documents, and financial summaries, then asks the model to synthesize everything into strategic priorities. The request sounds reasonable. The result is almost always shallow.

The model is not failing because it lacks capability. It is failing because the attention budget has been spread so thin across so many documents and objectives that no single area receives sufficient allocative depth to produce rigorous analysis.

The solution is phased analysis — breaking the saturated task into sequential focused sessions, each with a compressed handoff to the next:

```
PHASED APPROACH TO SATURATED INPUT:

Phase 1 Session: Extract risk indicators from Q1-
Q3 performance reports only.
Handoff block: [3 key risk indicators identified,
with supporting evidence]

Phase 2 Session: Extract contractual exposure
from supplied agreements only.
Handoff block: [2 material contractual risks
identified]

Phase 3 Session: Using Phase 1 and Phase 2
findings only, synthesize Q3 strategic
priorities.
Input: Compressed handoff blocks from Phases 1
and 2. No raw documents.

Result: Each phase operates at full analytical
depth. The synthesis phase works from high-
quality compressed findings rather than low-
quality raw volume.
```

7.11 The Cognitive Compression Loop

One of the most interesting emergent effects of disciplined token management is that operators themselves begin changing.

As users develop session architecture skills, they typically find that their thinking becomes more operationally precise. Constructing a front-loaded system prompt forces clarity about what the session is actually for. Building a Handoff Block forces clarity about what was actually learned. Designing phased workflows forces clarity about how the problem actually decomposes.

Natural CodeLex calls this the Cognitive Compression Loop: the feedback system in which AI workflow discipline progressively trains operators toward greater communicative and analytical precision. The AI shapes the operator's thinking habits. The operator, in turn, designs better AI environments.

Organizations that develop strong prompt architecture culture consistently report a secondary benefit: internal communication improves. The same discipline that produces clean AI prompts — stating objectives clearly, separating constraints from goals, specifying what success looks like — produces clearer human communication in meetings, documents, and decisions.

Token discipline is not just a technical optimization. It is a cognitive discipline that compounds.

Final Principle: Treat Every Token as a Decision

The operators who never hit context limits are not the ones using the most powerful models. They are the ones who treat every token as a deliberate allocation decision — who have learned that the quality of AI output is often determined less by what is added to the prompt and more by what is removed from it.

Structural compression, session segmentation, front-loaded system prompts, compressed handoff blocks, and shorthand frameworks are not technical tricks. They are the practical infrastructure of cognitive economy — the discipline of doing more with less that separates operators who work with AI from operators who work inside it.

Because attention is finite. And every token you waste on noise is a token that cannot do work.

CHAPTER 8

THE FAILURE OF LINEAR THINKING

Recursive Intelligence and Multi-Path Reasoning

Traditional computing trained humans toward a deeply linear model of information processing: input a query, receive an answer, act on the answer. This workflow was appropriate for the deterministic, retrieval-based systems that dominated computing for fifty years. It is fundamentally inappropriate for probabilistic AI systems that perform best when used recursively, comparatively, and iteratively.

The failure of linear thinking in AI contexts is not a user failure — it is a mismatch between mental model and system architecture. Users who approach AI with the mental model appropriate for a search engine or a calculator consistently produce weaker outputs than users who approach it as a probabilistic system that benefits from structured recursion. The difference in outcome is not marginal. For complex analytical tasks, recursive workflows routinely produce outputs that are categorically more sophisticated than those generated through single-pass interaction.

This chapter develops a systematic understanding of recursive intelligence — why single-pass thinking fails, how recursive structures improve analytical quality, what specific architectures produce reliable improvements, and how to avoid the specific failure modes that recursive workflows introduce.

8.1 Why Single-Pass Thinking Fails for Complex Problems

For simple, well-defined problems, single-pass generation works adequately. A question with a clear answer — a definition, a calculation, a straightforward factual query —

does not benefit significantly from recursive analysis. The linear model is appropriate.

For complex problems — strategic decisions, multi-variable risk analyses, organizational diagnoses, scenario planning — single-pass generation has structural limitations that recursive architectures address:

PREMATURE CONVERGENCE: Linear generation commits to an analytical direction early, consistently elaborating within it. The analytical territory covered in the first few sentences shapes everything that follows. Alternative framings, competing explanations, and contradictory evidence that would have been surfaced by a different initial direction remain invisible. The output appears comprehensive because it is internally consistent — but it may be comprehensively wrong because it committed to the wrong initial direction.

CONFIRMATION DYNAMICS: Once the model has generated an initial analysis, subsequent generation within the same session tends to reinforce rather than challenge it. The probability distribution shifts toward 'what is consistent with what I have said' rather than 'what is true regardless of what I have said.' This creates a form of analytical self-confirmation that compounds with each additional exchange.

PERSPECTIVE BLINDNESS: Single-pass generation produces analysis from the most statistically available perspective given the prompt's framing. A question about organizational risk framed in financial terms will receive a financial analysis. The operational risks, the people risks, and the regulatory risks that a different framing would have surfaced remain invisible — not because the model cannot analyze them, but because the linear framing never directed it to.

Recursive intelligence addresses all three limitations by structuring the generation process so that multiple analytical passes, multiple perspectives, and explicit challenge cycles are embedded in the workflow architecture rather than depending on single-pass comprehensiveness.

8.2 The Recursive Workflow Architecture

The following architecture provides a systematic structure for recursive analysis that consistently produces higher-quality outputs than single-pass generation for complex problems:

```
RECURSIVE ANALYSIS WORKFLOW

PHASE 1 — INITIAL GENERATION
Generate analysis from primary perspective and
primary analytical framework.
Constraints: Do not self-qualify or hedge.
Generate the strongest version of the analysis
the evidence supports. Premature hedging weakens
the adversarial phases.
Output: Initial findings, conclusions,
recommendations.

          ↓ [Diagnostic review: What assumptions
does Phase 1 make? What perspectives did it not
consider?]

PHASE 2 — ADVERSARIAL CRITIQUE
Explicitly challenge Phase 1 output.
Instruction: 'Challenge the previous analysis.
For each major conclusion: identify the primary
assumption it depends on, identify a plausible
scenario in which that assumption fails, and
identify one alternative explanation the analysis
underweighted.'
Output: Specific challenges to specific
conclusions. Not general skepticism — targeted
identification of analytical vulnerabilities.

          ↓ [Diagnostic review: Do the Phase 2
challenges reveal genuine gaps or superficial
alternatives?]

PHASE 3 — ALTERNATIVE PATH GENERATION
Generate competing analytical frameworks for the
same problem.
Instruction: 'Generate two alternative
interpretations of this situation that would lead
to substantially different conclusions. For each:
identify supporting evidence, identify evidence
that contradicts it, and rate plausibility.'
```

```
Output: 2-3 competing analytical frameworks with
explicit evidence evaluation.

          ↓ [Diagnostic review: Where do Phase 1
and Phase 3 frameworks converge? Where do they
diverge? What explains the divergence?]

PHASE 4 — COMPARATIVE SYNTHESIS
Evaluate Phase 1 findings against Phase 2
challenges and Phase 3 alternatives.
Instruction: 'Synthesize the previous analyses.
Where Phase 1 and Phase 3 converge, treat
conclusions as higher-confidence. Where they
diverge, explain the divergence and what
additional information would resolve it. Where
Phase 2 identified genuine vulnerabilities,
revise conclusions accordingly.'
Output: Synthesis with explicit confidence
calibration.

          ↓ [Diagnostic review: Is the synthesis
actionable? Does it preserve genuine uncertainty
rather than resolving it artificially?]

PHASE 5 — COMPRESSION AND DECISION FRAMING
Compress synthesis into decision-ready format.
Instruction: 'Compress the synthesis into an
executive decision brief. Preserve confidence
levels. Flag remaining uncertainties explicitly
as decision-critical unknowns rather than
resolving them with false precision.'
Output: Final analysis with assumption
transparency and remaining uncertainty clearly
identified.
```

This architecture is more investment than a single-pass prompt. For simple or low-stakes problems, the investment is not justified. For complex or high-stakes problems — strategic decisions, significant financial commitments, organizational changes, risk assessments — the improvement in analytical quality typically justifies the additional work substantially.

8.3 Real Scenario: Acquisition Decision Under Recursion

The following demonstrates recursive intelligence applied to a realistic strategic decision:

```
SCENARIO: A mid-market private equity firm is
evaluating a $45M acquisition of a regional
logistics company. Initial financial modeling
suggests strong strategic fit and achievable
synergies.

PHASE 1 — INITIAL ANALYSIS:

'The acquisition presents strong strategic value.
The target's regional network complements the
portfolio's existing coverage gaps in the
southeastern market. Revenue synergies of $8-12M
are achievable within 18 months through combined
customer cross-selling. Management team is
experienced. Integration risk is moderate given
operational compatibility. Recommended: proceed
with full due diligence at current valuation.'

On its own, this reads as competent, confident,
actionable analysis. It is exactly the kind of
output a linear workflow would accept and act on.

PHASE 2 — ADVERSARIAL CRITIQUE:

Prompt: 'Challenge every conclusion in the
previous analysis. For each, identify the
assumption it depends on and a scenario in which
that assumption fails.'

Critique output:
- 'Revenue synergies of $8-12M' — ASSUMPTION:
Cross-selling opportunity exists and is
achievable within current sales infrastructure.
FAILURE SCENARIO: Customer overlap between
portfolio and target is actually high, making
cross-sell opportunity much smaller than assumed.
Customer base analysis required before synergy
estimates can be validated.
- '18 months' timeline — ASSUMPTION: Integration
can proceed without operational disruption.
FAILURE SCENARIO: Logistics operations require
significant system integration that creates
service disruption during the integration period,
damaging the customer relationships that create
the synergy value.
- 'Moderate integration risk' — ASSUMPTION:
Operational compatibility is actually comparable.
```

FAILURE SCENARIO: 'Operational compatibility' has not been defined or tested. Cultural differences between PE ownership model and regional family-owned operations are a documented failure pattern in this acquisition category.

- 'Experienced management team' — ASSUMPTION: Management will remain post-acquisition. FAILURE SCENARIO: Management retention has not been assessed. Regional family-owned operators frequently exit post-acquisition at exactly the moment their operational knowledge is most critical.

PHASE 3 — ALTERNATIVE INTERPRETATION:

Prompt: 'Generate an alternative analytical interpretation of this acquisition that reaches a substantially different conclusion. Identify its supporting evidence and any evidence that contradicts it.'

Alternative framework output:

'The acquisition may be attractively priced because it reflects genuine operational limitations rather than market undervaluation. The regional network 'complementarity' may reflect coverage in areas where the acquirer previously assessed and chose not to operate — meaning the strategic rationale may be weaker than assumed. The 'experienced management team' in a regional family business context typically means highly relationship-dependent operations that do not transfer cleanly to PE ownership. The 18-month synergy timeline is inconsistent with the integration timelines documented in comparable logistics acquisitions, which average 30–42 months to synergy realization.

Contradicting evidence: Target has maintained customer relationships for 12+ years (relationship stability indicator). Regional market has genuine coverage gap for acquirer. Financial fundamentals are sound.'

This alternative interpretation does not necessarily reach the right conclusion. But it surfaces specific risks that the initial analysis did not consider — including the acquisition-attractiveness paradox (attractively priced

```
because genuinely limited) and the synergy
timeline gap.

PHASE 4 — SYNTHESIS:

Convergence (higher confidence):
- Regional network has genuine strategic value
- Financial fundamentals support the valuation
basis
- Customer relationship stability is a genuine
positive indicator

Divergence requiring resolution:
- Synergy timeline: Initial analysis (18 months)
vs. comparable transaction data (30–42 months).
Decision-critical: 18-month vs. 36-month synergy
timeline changes NPV significantly.
- Management retention: Not assessed in initial
analysis. Now identified as potentially
acquisition-blocking.
- Customer overlap: Initial analysis assumes low
overlap (high cross-sell opportunity). Must be
verified before synergy estimates are defensible.

Revised conclusion: Due diligence should
prioritize management retention commitment,
customer base overlap analysis, and comparable
transaction synergy timelines. Current
recommendation: conditional — proceed with due
diligence, but treat valuation as unvalidated
until these three questions are answered.
```

The recursive workflow did not simply generate more analysis. It identified three specific decision-critical unknowns that the initial analysis normalized — unknowns that, if answered unfavorably, would each independently change the investment recommendation. A single-pass workflow would have provided the initial analysis and no more. The recursive workflow provides the initial analysis and a map of where it might be wrong.

8.4 Comparative Reasoning and Multi-Path Analysis

One of the most valuable recursive techniques for complex analytical problems is comparative reasoning — the practice of forcing the model to generate and evaluate multiple competing interpretations simultaneously rather than committing to a single analytical direction.

Human decision-making is vulnerable to a well-documented cognitive failure called anchoring: the tendency to give disproportionate weight to the first piece of information encountered, and to evaluate all subsequent information relative to that anchor. In AI workflows, single-pass generation replicates this failure — the initial analytical direction functions as an anchor that shapes all subsequent generation.

Comparative reasoning breaks the anchor by requiring multiple independent analytical paths before synthesis:

```
COMPARATIVE REASONING INSTRUCTION:

Generate THREE competing explanations for [the
observed phenomenon].

For each explanation:
1. State the core causal mechanism
2. Identify the specific evidence that supports
it
3. Identify the specific evidence that
contradicts it
4. Estimate the probability that this explanation
is primarily correct (as a percentage, with
reasoning)

Do not attempt to reconcile the explanations at
this stage. Develop each independently to its
strongest form before evaluating them
comparatively.
```

The instruction to develop each explanation 'to its strongest form before evaluating comparatively' is critical. Premature reconciliation — the attempt to integrate multiple perspectives before they have been fully developed — typically produces hybrid outputs that are weaker than any of the individual perspectives would have been. The value of comparative reasoning comes from the tension between well-developed competing explanations, not from their premature synthesis.

8.5 Recursive Hallucination Risk and Verification Gates

Recursive workflows introduce a specific failure mode that requires active management: Recursive Hallucination Amplification. An incorrect assumption that enters the workflow in Phase 1 can be progressively reinforced through adversarial critique (which identifies other vulnerabilities but may leave the original error intact), alternative interpretation (which provides a different wrong answer rather than the right one), and synthesis (which integrates both the wrong answer and its alternative into a coherent-seeming conclusion).

The result can be a highly sophisticated, internally consistent, structurally impressive analysis built on a false foundation — and precisely because of the adversarial critique and synthesis phases, it may seem more reliable than a simpler analysis that at least exposed its assumptions more visibly.

Verification gates are the primary defense against this failure mode:

```
VERIFICATION GATE — Insert between recursive
phases when factual accuracy is critical:

'Before proceeding to the next phase, identify
every factual claim in the previous analysis that
is not directly derivable from the provided
source material.

For each such claim:
1. Identify it explicitly
2. Label it as: reasonable inference / general
knowledge assumption / speculative assessment
3. Flag any claim in the reasonable inference or
speculative assessment categories that would
significantly change the conclusion if wrong

Proceed to the next phase using only claims that
are either source-supported or explicitly flagged
as requiring external verification.'
```

Verification gates interrupt the recursion cycle to ensure that analytical errors do not compound through successive phases. They are most valuable at the transition between Phase 1 and Phase 2 (before adversarial critique reinforces incorrect claims) and between Phase 3 and Phase 4 (before synthesis integrates errors from multiple analytical paths).

8.6 Recursive Fatigue and When to Stop

Recursive workflows have diminishing returns. The first adversarial phase typically produces substantial improvement in analytical quality. The second produces meaningful but smaller improvement. The third produces marginal improvement. The fourth produces noise.

Beyond a certain point, additional recursion stops improving analysis and begins generating analytical cycling — successive phases producing increasingly contradictory outputs without convergence, or increasingly similar outputs that add no new information. Both are signals that the recursion has reached or exceeded its productive limit.

The appropriate response to recursive fatigue is compression: a synthesis prompt that forces the workflow to consolidate current findings, resolve contradictions through explicit prioritization, acknowledge remaining genuine uncertainty rather than resolving it through additional analysis, and produce a final output that is ready for human review and decision.

The ability to recognize the recursion's productive limit and compress toward a decision-ready output is as important as the ability to design effective recursive structures. The operator who continues recursive cycling past the productive limit wastes resources and degrades output quality. The operator who compresses prematurely misses the analytical improvement that additional cycles would have provided. Calibrating the appropriate recursion depth for different problem types is a skill developed through practice.

Final Principle: Designing Reasoning Systems

Advanced prompting is not only about generating answers. For complex problems, it is about designing reasoning systems — structured workflows that produce analytical quality through recursive evaluation rather than single-pass generation.

Linear thinking collapses complexity prematurely, anchors on initial framings, and produces confident analysis of a single interpretation while leaving alternative interpretations unexplored. Recursive intelligence creates comparative analysis, adversarial review, branching logic, and deeper strategic visibility — not through any single sophisticated prompt, but through the architectural discipline of building workflows that evaluate conclusions rather than simply generating them.

The strongest AI operators are not the ones demanding immediate certainty. They are the ones capable of exploring alternatives, challenging assumptions, compressing noise, and refining conclusions recursively — until what remains is not just confident analysis, but analysis that has been tested against the specific ways it might be wrong.

CHAPTER 9

THE COLLAPSE OF SEARCH

AI as Cognitive Infrastructure

For most of human history, accessing knowledge required physical proximity to it. Knowledge lived in specific places — libraries, monasteries, universities, archives — and accessing it required traveling to those places, navigating their organizational systems, and doing the synthetic work of interpretation yourself. The burden of getting from information to understanding was entirely human.

The printing press changed the distribution of information without fundamentally changing the access model. Books could travel; knowledge could spread. But someone still had to read the books, compare them, evaluate their claims, and synthesize across them. The cognitive burden remained with the reader.

The internet radically changed information access. Search engines made it possible to find information on virtually any topic in seconds, from anywhere. The physical barriers collapsed. But the cognitive architecture remained surprisingly similar: the search engine found information; the human synthesized it. Google returns ten links; the user reads the links, compares the sources, evaluates the credibility, and constructs understanding manually. The navigational friction decreased. The synthetic burden did not.

Large language models represent a qualitative shift in this centuries-long trajectory. For the first time in mainstream computing history, users interact with systems that do not merely retrieve or surface information — they synthesize it. The user asks a question. The system generates a synthesized response that integrates, interprets, and organizes information rather than simply locating it.

This shift is what Natural CodeLex calls the Collapse of Search. Not the disappearance of search engines — they will continue to exist and serve specific needs. But the end of retrieval as the dominant paradigm for knowledge access. The interface between humans and information is becoming conversational, synthetic, and interpretive. The consequences of this transition extend far beyond productivity and convenience.

9.1 From Libraries to Search to Synthesis: The Trajectory

Understanding the significance of the current transition requires placing it in its historical sequence.

THE LIBRARY ERA: Knowledge access required physical presence, institutional membership, and significant navigational effort. The Dewey Decimal System and its predecessors were not merely organizational tools — they were the interface through which knowledge became accessible. Mastering those organizational systems was itself a form of expertise. Reference librarians were knowledge access professionals whose value lay in their navigational fluency. The cognitive synthesis — the actual work of understanding — happened entirely in the reader's mind.

THE SEARCH ENGINE ERA: Google's innovation was not merely making retrieval faster. It was making retrieval legible to natural language rather than requiring mastery of organizational systems. You no longer needed to know the Library of Congress Subject Headings to find information about organizational behavior — you could type 'why do companies fail' and receive relevant results. The search interface democratized information access by removing the navigational expertise requirement. But the synthetic burden remained. You received links; you did the reading. You received sources; you did the comparison. You received information; you constructed understanding.

THE SYNTHESIS ERA: AI systems compress the gap between information and understanding. The user asks a question in natural language. The system generates a synthesized response that has already performed the integration, comparison, and interpretation that the search era left to the user. The synthetic burden shifts from human to machine. This is historically unprecedented, and its implications compound as the technology scales.

9.2 Epistemic Compression: What Synthesis Removes

Every synthesis involves tradeoffs. The compression of large amounts of information into a synthesized response necessarily removes something. Understanding what synthesis removes — and what that removal costs — is essential for operators who want to use AI synthesis intelligently rather than naively.

NUANCE AND EDGE CASES: When fifty articles are compressed into a synthesized overview, the edge cases that appeared in articles 23 and 47 disappear. The anomalous finding that only one source reported is statistically insignificant at the synthesis level and gets smoothed over by the weight of sources that reported differently. The minority perspective that one careful analyst emphasized becomes invisible in the synthesis. The synthesis produces the median view, not the full distribution of views.

METHODOLOGICAL CONTEXT: Original sources carry framing about their own limitations. A study notes its sample size, its geographic restriction, its methodological caveats. Synthesis strips these qualifications in favor of the finding. 'A study found a modest correlation with significant limitations and a small sample size' becomes 'research shows' in synthesis. The epistemic quality of the claim degrades without any change in the apparent confidence with which it is expressed.

SOURCE TRANSPARENCY: When a synthesized response integrates information from multiple sources, the provenance of specific claims typically disappears. The user cannot trace which source supports which claim, cannot evaluate the relative credibility of different sources, and cannot identify where consensus ends and contested territory begins. The synthesis presents an integrated view without the navigational transparency that would allow a careful user to evaluate it.

INTERPRETIVE AUTHORITY CONCENTRATION: Perhaps most significantly, synthesis concentrates interpretive authority. When millions of people receive synthesized responses to their questions through the same AI system, the interpretive choices embedded in that synthesis — what to include, how to frame it, what to emphasize — gain outsized influence over collective understanding. The same framing choices that were previously distributed across thousands of independent sources become concentrated in a single synthesis infrastructure.

Advanced operators use synthesis as a starting point rather than a terminus — as acceleration for the analytical process rather than a replacement for it. The synthesized response provides scaffolding; the human operator provides the critical evaluation, source verification, and independent judgment that synthesis cannot supply.

9.3 The Death of Navigation and Its Cognitive Consequences

The search era required navigation. Users had to search, compare, filter, follow links, evaluate sources, synthesize across multiple documents, and make continuous judgments about relevance and credibility. This process was effortful. It was also cognitively valuable in ways that are only becoming visible as the navigation requirement disappears.

Navigational search created friction that forced active cognitive engagement. The act of reading and comparing multiple sources — even when inefficient — produced the kind of repeated exposure and active processing that supports deep comprehension and durable memory. The struggle of navigating between incompatible sources required the user to develop and apply evaluation criteria, building the epistemic muscles that sophisticated information use requires.

Research on GPS navigation provides an instructive parallel. Studies consistently show that users who rely on GPS navigation develop weaker spatial memory and spatial reasoning skills than users who navigate using maps or direct route-learning. The GPS does the navigational work; the human follows instructions. The skill that requires practice to develop — spatial reasoning from a network representation — goes unpracticed and weakens.

If AI synthesis does something analogous for analytical reasoning — if the habit of having sources synthesized for you reduces the practice of doing the synthesis yourself — the cognitive consequences may extend beyond the immediate convenience. The capacity for deep analytical engagement with primary sources, the ability to evaluate competing interpretations without external guidance, and the tolerance for the productive friction of encountering difficult material without immediate synthesis may all be skills that require sustained practice to maintain.

This is not an argument against AI synthesis. The productivity gains are real, and the accessibility improvements for people who previously had no viable path to the knowledge they needed are genuinely valuable. It is an argument for deliberate cognitive discipline — for maintaining the analytical practices that AI convenience creates pressure to abandon, because those practices produce cognitive capabilities that AI convenience cannot replicate.

9.4 Enterprise Knowledge Synthesis: Efficiency and Risks

Inside organizations, AI synthesis is already displacing internal search as the primary knowledge access mechanism — with efficiency gains that are substantial and risks that are underappreciated.

```
ENTERPRISE SYNTHESIS SCENARIO — QUARTERLY
OPERATIONS REVIEW

TRADITIONAL WORKFLOW:
```

An operations director preparing for a quarterly board presentation needs to synthesize performance data across four regional operations.

- Requests reports from four regional managers (3-5 days)
- Reviews each report manually (2-3 hours)
- Identifies cross-regional patterns and anomalies (2-3 hours)
- Drafts synthesis for board presentation (3-4 hours)
- Total elapsed time: 5-7 days, 8-12 active hours

AI-MEDIATED WORKFLOW:
Operations director uploads four regional reports to AI system with structured synthesis prompt.

- AI synthesizes cross-regional patterns and anomalies (3-5 minutes)
- Director reviews synthesis and validates key findings (45-60 minutes)
- Director refines and contextualizes for board presentation (1-2 hours)
- Total elapsed time: 1-2 days, 2-3 active hours

EFFICIENCY GAIN: 70-80% reduction in active time. Real and significant.

RISK INTRODUCED:
The AI synthesis may miss the anomalous finding in the Northeast regional report — the one where a specific customer segment showed early churn signals not yet reflected in aggregate metrics. The anomaly was present in the data, but it was a low-frequency pattern in a single region that the synthesis weighted appropriately relative to the larger patterns — which means it weighted it too low for an operations director who knows this particular customer segment is strategically critical.

The traditional workflow, which required the director to read each report individually, would have caught this anomaly because the director's domain knowledge would have made it salient. The AI synthesis, which had no access to that domain knowledge about strategic priorities, compressed it away.

```
CONCLUSION: The efficiency gain is real. The risk
is also real. The appropriate response is not to
abandon AI synthesis but to design review
workflows that combine AI synthesis efficiency
with human domain-knowledge-guided anomaly
detection.
```

The enterprise synthesis challenge is fundamentally a workflow design problem: how do you capture the efficiency gains of AI synthesis while preserving the human judgment and domain knowledge that make synthesis genuinely useful rather than merely fast? The organizations that solve this design problem will have substantial competitive advantages over those that either resist AI synthesis entirely or adopt it without adequate verification architecture.

9.5 The Risk of Synthetic Authority

Among the risks introduced by the Collapse of Search, Synthetic Authority — the tendency to grant unearned credibility to AI-generated content by virtue of its structural sophistication — may be the most consequential and the least visible.

AI systems produce language that consistently mimics the structural hallmarks of expertise: organized argument, measured qualification, apparent comprehensiveness, professional vocabulary, logical sequencing. These features have historically been reliable proxies for the cognitive investment required to produce them — producing expert-looking analysis required expert knowledge, or at minimum significant intellectual effort. In a world where these surface features can be generated instantly for any position on any topic, the proxy becomes unreliable.

The danger is not primarily that AI outputs will be obviously wrong. Obvious errors are easy to catch. The danger is that AI outputs will be subtly wrong — containing framing choices that systematically distort the analysis, analytical errors that require domain expertise to identify, confident assertions built on unverified foundations — while displaying every surface feature that signals reliability.

This creates what might be called the Coherence Trap: the more internally consistent and professionally structured an AI output appears, the more likely a user is to accept it without critical examination — at precisely the moment when critical examination is most necessary. Incoherent, obviously flawed outputs trigger skepticism. Coherent, apparently sophisticated outputs suppress it. But coherence is a feature of the generation process, not a guarantee of the analytical quality of the content generated.

The appropriate response is not blanket skepticism toward all AI outputs, which would eliminate the genuine value they provide. It is calibrated skepticism — skepticism proportionate to the stakes of the decision being informed, the domain where AI synthesis is least reliable (recent events, highly technical domains, contested empirical questions), and the degree to which the output structure has been independently verified against primary sources.

9.6 The Human Skill Shift

As AI systems absorb more retrieval and synthesis functions, the skills that produce human economic and cognitive value shift accordingly. This shift is not uniform across all capabilities.

AI synthesis is becoming highly capable at: information compression and summarization, pattern identification across structured data, generating frameworks and analytical structures, producing the first draft of complex outputs, synthesizing across multiple sources within a defined scope.

AI synthesis remains limited for: evaluating the quality and credibility of sources (it can identify them, not reliably evaluate them), navigating genuinely novel or rapidly evolving situations where training data is thin, applying deep domain knowledge that is tacit rather than documented, making value judgments that require accountability and consequence-awareness, and identifying the specific anomalies that domain expertise makes salient.

Human value in an AI-mediated environment centers increasingly on judgment, source evaluation, anomaly detection through domain knowledge, verification of synthetic outputs, and the accountability that AI systems cannot assume. This does not make domain expertise less valuable — it makes the combination of domain expertise and AI fluency dramatically more valuable than either alone.

The human who can direct AI synthesis intelligently, evaluate its outputs critically, identify where it fails, and apply the domain knowledge that makes specific anomalies visible is substantially more capable than either the human without AI tools or the AI system without human domain knowledge and judgment.

9.7 A Real Failure: The Confident Wrong Answer

The following pattern has been documented across multiple enterprise financial analysis deployments.

A regional investment advisory firm began using AI synthesis for preliminary due diligence on acquisition targets. The workflow seemed to work well. Analysts uploaded financial filings, the AI produced structured summaries, and preliminary investment theses were developed faster than before.

On one occasion, the AI produced a synthesis that included a specific claim about a target company's revenue concentration — stating that no single customer represented more than 12% of revenue, and citing this as a positive risk indicator. The claim was wrong. It was a hallucination — the model had generated a plausible-sounding statistic not present in the uploaded filings. In fact, one customer represented approximately 34% of revenue, and that customer had publicly announced plans to bring the relevant service in-house.

The error was not caught during internal review. The synthesis was coherent, structured, and professionally formatted. The specific revenue concentration figure sounded precise — precise figures feel authoritative. The claim passed through preliminary analysis and informed the initial valuation model. It was caught six weeks later during independent outside-counsel due diligence, after the firm had already spent significant resources developing the investment thesis.

The forensic analysis was instructive. The AI had been given multiple financial documents to synthesize. One document mentioned customer diversification in general terms without providing specific figures. The model, generating the most statistically plausible continuation of a due diligence summary, produced a specific figure — because due diligence summaries typically contain specific figures in that position. Sentence structure plausibility overwhelmed the absence of underlying evidence.

This is the Coherence Trap at its most dangerous: wrong in exactly the form that a correct answer would have taken. The fix required three changes: a source constraint requiring every numerical claim to be traceable to a specific document and page; a verification gate asking the model to identify claims it could not source; and a human review protocol targeting numerical claims specifically. The lesson: fluent outputs require more verification discipline than rough ones, not less.

Final Principle: Synthesis Requires Stewardship

The Collapse of Search is not simply a productivity improvement. It is a cognitive shift — a change in the relationship between humans and knowledge that is as structurally significant as the introduction of printing or the creation of the internet.

The shift creates extraordinary leverage: dramatically accelerated access to synthesized understanding, reduced friction for learning and analysis, improved accessibility for people previously excluded from knowledge access by navigational barriers.

It also creates dependency, epistemic compression risk, Synthetic Authority, and the potential for gradual atrophy of the analytical skills that synthesis convenience makes it easy to stop practicing.

The future of intelligent engagement with an AI-mediated information environment belongs not to the people who access the most synthesized information, but to the people who understand how to guide synthesis intelligently, evaluate its outputs critically, preserve the domain expertise and analytical habits that synthesis cannot replicate, and maintain the cognitive sovereignty to question what the synthesis tells them.

Because once search collapses into synthesis, the interface between humans and knowledge changes permanently. How we steward that interface — with what combination of enthusiasm for its possibilities and discipline about its limitations — will shape the quality of collective understanding that human civilization can sustain.

CHAPTER 10

SYNTHETIC LABOR AND THE ACCELERATION

AI as Workforce Multiplication — and What Comes Next

For most of the industrial era, organizational productivity was roughly proportional to organizational headcount. If you needed more output, you hired more people. If you needed faster decision support, you built larger analytical infrastructure. The relationship between labor and output was linear — departures from linearity were explained by management quality, process efficiency, and technology adoption, not by any fundamental change in the labor-output relationship itself.

AI systems are disrupting that relationship — not by replacing human intelligence wholesale, but by compressing the amount of labor required to produce specific categories of cognitive output. Tasks that previously required team-weeks of professional effort can increasingly be accomplished in operator-hours with AI assistance. The compression is not uniform across all task types. But where it applies, it creates leverage asymmetries that have significant economic and organizational implications.

Natural CodeLex calls this transformation Synthetic Labor: the restructuring of cognitive work through AI-mediated compression of coordination, synthesis, analysis, drafting, and operational throughput.

But understanding Synthetic Labor fully today requires something more than a productivity analysis. It requires understanding why AI capability is accelerating at the rate it is — and where that acceleration is pointing. Because the compression operators are experiencing today is not the ceiling. It may not even be the middle.

10.1 Where AI Compression Works: Before and After

The following demonstrates AI compression across representative enterprise workflows — with honest accounting of what remains human-dependent:

```
WORKFLOW 1 — COMPETITIVE INTELLIGENCE ANALYSIS

BEFORE AI:
2 senior analysts, 5–7 days. Manual review of
competitor communications, financial disclosures,
industry reports, analyst commentary. Pattern
identification across sources. Drafting, review,
revision cycles.
Approximate effort: 200–280 analyst-hours.

WITH AI ASSISTANCE:
1 operator, 1–2 days. Structured AI synthesis
across uploaded documents. Iterative refinement
for analytical depth. Human review and validation
of key findings.
Approximate effort: 16–24 operator-hours.
Compression ratio: approximately 10–12:1.

What compression does not eliminate: Strategic
judgment about what competitive dynamics actually
mean for this specific organization. The anomaly
detection that domain expertise makes salient.
Accountability.

WORKFLOW 2 — CONTRACT REVIEW AND RISK ASSESSMENT

BEFORE AI:
Experienced attorney, 6–8 hours per complex
commercial agreement.

WITH AI ASSISTANCE:
AI-assisted extraction with identity-framed risk
analysis. Attorney review focused on flagged
items only.
Approximate effort: 1.5–2.5 hours per agreement.
Compression ratio: approximately 3–5:1.

What compression does not eliminate: Legal
judgment on the significance and negotiability of
specific risks. Counterparty knowledge.
Professional accountability.
```

```
WORKFLOW 3 — STRATEGIC PLANNING PREPARATION

BEFORE AI:
Strategy team, 3–4 weeks for annual planning
cycle.

WITH AI ASSISTANCE:
Strategy team, 1–2 weeks with AI-accelerated
research synthesis and scenario development.
Compression ratio: approximately 2–3:1.

What compression does not eliminate:
Organizational knowledge about what assumptions
are realistic. Political judgment about what the
organization can execute. Relationship
intelligence.
```

AI compression is most powerful for information-intensive work requiring synthesis across large volumes of material, pattern identification in structured data, and first-draft production. It is least powerful for work requiring deep organizational context, tacit professional knowledge, political judgment, and accountability.

10.2 What AI Cannot Compress: The Honest Accounting

```
ORGANIZATIONAL POLITICS AND INFORMAL POWER:
Every organization has a formal structure and an
informal one. The informal structure — who
actually influences decisions, whose objections
can block initiatives, what coalitions are
required — exists in human relationships, not in
any document. AI synthesis cannot access it.

TRUST AND RELATIONSHIP CREDIBILITY:
Professional trust is built through demonstrated
reliability, shared history, and the
interpersonal dynamics of working through
difficult situations. It cannot be synthesized.
The advisor trusted because of a decade of
accurate judgment holds leverage that AI-assisted
analysis cannot replicate.

NEGOTIATION AND REAL-TIME READING:
```

```
High-stakes negotiation requires real-time
reading of counterparty signals, strategic
ambiguity, and interpersonal positioning that
unfolds in the room. AI can prepare the strategy.
It cannot execute the negotiation.

ACCOUNTABILITY AND PROFESSIONAL CONSEQUENCE:
Organizations require humans who can be held
responsible for consequential decisions. AI
outputs cannot accept accountability. Someone
must answer when the analysis is wrong.

TACIT AND EXPERIENTIAL KNOWLEDGE:
The accumulated pattern recognition professionals
develop through years of consequential decisions
— the sense that something is off about a deal, a
hire, a strategy — lives in human cognition. It
cannot be synthesized because it has never been
fully articulated.

EMOTIONAL INTELLIGENCE AND HUMAN DYNAMICS:
Leadership, conflict resolution, motivation, and
organizational culture development require
genuine emotional engagement with other human
beings. These are not secondary activities. They
are often the primary drivers of organizational
performance.
```

10.3 Organizational Resistance: The Structural Reality

The narrative of rapid, universal AI adoption underestimates the structural forces that slow, constrain, and in some cases prevent it — not through irrational resistance but through legitimate institutional function.

Regulated industries — financial services, healthcare, legal services, pharmaceuticals — operate under compliance frameworks built around human authorization for consequential decisions. AI may accelerate the analytical work; regulatory frameworks typically still require human sign-off. Changing those frameworks requires demonstrating reliability at a standard that takes years to establish.

Professional liability structures create similar friction. When AI-assisted legal advice is wrong, who is liable? When AI-assisted medical analysis misses a diagnosis, how is responsibility allocated? These questions are being resolved through litigation, regulation, and institutional policy — on timescales measured in years.

Cultural resistance is also real. Professional identity is partly built on cognitive labor. Professionals whose value proposition rested on analytical thoroughness may experience AI adoption as a threat to the competency foundation of their professional identity. This is not mere irrationality. It is a rational response to genuine disruption.

10.4 The Governance Imperative: Scaling Failure

The same compression that makes synthetic labor powerful makes its failure modes consequential at organizational scale.

Traditional cognitive workflows had natural friction that created error-checking opportunities. Multiple humans reviewing the same analysis created redundant verification. The time required for manual synthesis allowed reflection. Coordination overhead, though inefficient, introduced natural review points. The organizational processes AI compression displaces were not merely inefficient — they were, unintentionally, verification architectures.

AI-compressed workflows reduce this friction significantly. A flawed assumption entering an AI analysis workflow can propagate through multiple downstream decisions before human review catches it. The organization that compresses twenty analyst-hours into two AI-assisted hours has not eliminated the need for analytical rigor. It has concentrated the risk of analytical failure into a smaller window that requires proportionally more careful oversight.

10.5 Why AI Is Accelerating Exponentially

Something has changed in the development trajectory of AI systems that operators today must understand. The pace of capability improvement is not following a standard technology adoption curve. It is accelerating in ways that have no clear historical precedent — and the reason is structural, not incidental.

AI is now helping build AI.

This single fact changes everything about how capability development should be understood. In every prior technological era, the tools used to build new technology were fundamentally different from the technology being built. Engineers designed semiconductor fabrication equipment using conventional engineering tools. Software developers wrote operating systems using earlier programming languages and compilers. The tools and the output were distinct categories.

In the current AI era, that separation has collapsed. Large language models are being used to generate training data for the next generation of large language models. AI systems are writing significant portions of the code used to build AI systems. AI is running evaluations of AI outputs, proposing architectural improvements, identifying failure modes, and accelerating the research cycles that produce new capabilities.

The loop is closing. The system is becoming part of its own development infrastructure. And when a system contributes to building a more capable version of itself, which then contributes to building a still more capable version, the compounding rate is no longer constrained by the pace at which human researchers can work. It is constrained only by compute, data, and the rate at which each generation can meaningfully improve on the previous one.

Today, that rate has not plateaued. The evidence suggests it is still climbing.

10.6 The AI-Assists-AI Loop: What It Means Operationally

For operators, the AI-assists-AI dynamic has immediate practical implications that extend beyond abstract concern about exponential progress.

The first implication is that the workflows operators design today will become obsolete faster than any prior generation of professional tools. A workflow optimized for current AI capability will need to be rethought — not because it stopped working, but because the system it was designed for has been superseded by a substantially more capable successor. The half-life of AI workflow optimization is shortening.

The second implication is that the gap between operators who continuously adapt and those who do not is widening at a faster rate than in prior technological transitions. In the software era, a professional who learned strong digital skills in 1995 could maintain reasonable currency through 2005 with modest updating. The AI era does not appear to offer the same stability window. The pace of capability change means that operator skills developed for today's systems may require significant updating within two to three years — not ten.

The third implication is more subtle but perhaps most important. As AI systems become better at AI development, the specific technical knowledge required to understand the systems at a deep level is increasingly held by the AI systems themselves rather than by human researchers. This creates a growing knowledge asymmetry: the systems are outpacing human ability to fully characterize their own behavior. Understanding what AI systems do — precisely, reliably, mechanistically — is becoming harder even as using them becomes easier.

For operators, this means that the verification discipline emphasized throughout this book becomes more important, not less, as systems become more capable. A system you cannot fully characterize should not be trusted without verification, regardless of how impressive its outputs appear.

10.7 Introducing ARI: Artificial Reasoning Intelligence

The capability trajectory of AI systems points toward a transitional stage that has not yet been clearly named or defined in mainstream discourse. Natural CodeLex introduces a term for it: ARI — Artificial Reasoning Intelligence.

ARI is not current AI. It is not ASI. It is the conceptual stage between them — the point at which AI systems transition from probabilistic synthesis to genuine reasoning: the capacity for multi-step logical inference, hypothesis formation, self-correction through understanding rather than pattern approximation, and — most distinctively — something functionally equivalent to common sense.

Understanding what ARI's common sense would actually consist of requires rethinking what human common sense actually is.

10.8 What Common Sense Actually Is

Human beings tend to think of common sense as a property of individual minds — the capacity to reason practically and reliably about everyday situations. But on examination, common sense is not primarily an individual property. It is a social and distributed one.

Common sense is what most people, operating from similar experience and similar reasoning patterns, independently arrive at. A thing is obvious when enough minds have processed similar information through similar cognitive frameworks and converged on the same conclusion. The convergence is what makes it common. The independent arrival is what gives it epistemic weight.

This framing illuminates something that is normally obscured: visionaries, artists, inventors, and genuine originals are not wrong. They are early. Their reasoning has not yet been adopted widely enough to become common. Their conclusions sit outside the current convergence boundary — which is what makes them look like outliers rather than pioneers.

Galileo's model of the solar system was not a crazy idea. It was a correct idea that had not yet gathered the consensus weight required to become obvious. The Wright brothers were not delusional. They were running ahead of the convergence curve. Every transformative idea in human history followed this pattern: fringe before adoption, obvious after it.

The speed of adoption determines how long a correct idea remains 'crazy.' When adoption is slow — measured in generations — visionaries may die before their ideas become common sense. When adoption accelerates — as it has in the internet era — the gap between fringe and obvious compresses from decades to years. In the AI era, it may compress further still.

10.9 ARI's Common Sense: Consensus Cognition at Scale

What Natural CodeLex proposes is that ARI systems will develop something functionally equivalent to common sense not through individual reasoning sophistication, but through multi-agent consensus cognition — a mechanism that mirrors the distributed social process through which human common sense actually emerges.

The architecture looks like this: rather than a single model generating a single output, ARI systems involve multiple reasoning agents independently processing the same problem through different frameworks, checking each other's conclusions, challenging each other's assumptions, and converging on answers that survive multi-perspective scrutiny. The convergence is what carries epistemic weight. An answer that multiple independent reasoning agents arrive at through different paths is more reliable than any single agent's conclusion — for the same reason that a fact independently confirmed by multiple unrelated sources is more reliable than a single source.

This is not a hypothetical architecture. It is already present in primitive form. Constitutional AI systems use multiple evaluators to check outputs against principles. Ensemble methods combine multiple model outputs to reduce variance. Chain-of-thought verification asks models to check their own reasoning. These are early, limited implementations of the same underlying principle — that distributed independent reasoning produces more reliable conclusions than single-pass generation.

ARI extends this principle to genuine reasoning rather than pattern completion. The defining characteristic of ARI — what makes it distinct from current AI — is that its multi-agent consensus process would operate on the level of logical inference rather than statistical approximation. Agents would not be averaging outputs across probability distributions. They would be checking each other's reasoning chains, identifying logical errors, proposing alternative hypotheses, and converging on conclusions that are robust to challenge rather than merely plausible.

```
CURRENT AI (Probabilistic Synthesis):
Generation: Statistical pattern completion across
learned distributions.
Common sense equivalent: None. Plausibility, not
correctness.
Failure mode: Confident hallucination – plausible
output that is wrong.

ARI (Artificial Reasoning Intelligence):
Generation: Multi-agent consensus reasoning
across logical inference chains.
Common sense equivalent: Convergent conclusions
that survive independent multi-perspective
challenge.
Failure mode: Disagreement without resolution –
agents that cannot converge signal genuine
uncertainty.

ASI (Artificial Superintelligence):
Generation: Beyond current characterization.
Common sense equivalent: Unknown – potentially
alien to human intuition in some domains.
Failure mode: Unknown – which is itself the
central governance concern.
```

10.10 What ARI Changes for Operators

The operator relationship with ARI systems would be fundamentally different from the operator relationship with current AI — and understanding that difference is essential for operators designing workflows that will remain relevant through the transition.

With current AI, the operator directs a probabilistic synthesis engine. The system generates plausible continuations. The operator evaluates, iterates, and refines. The intelligence is primarily in the operator's architectural choices — the prompt design, the constraint structure, the iteration strategy. The system is powerful, but it is not reasoning. It is completing patterns with sophisticated fluency.

With ARI systems, the operator relationship begins to shift toward genuine collaboration. A system capable of multi-step reasoning, hypothesis formation, and self-correction through understanding is not merely completing the operator's instructions — it is engaging with the problem. It can challenge the operator's framing. It can identify logical errors in the operator's assumptions. It can pursue reasoning paths that the operator did not specify because the reasoning itself generated them.

This is qualitatively different. And it changes what operator skill means.

The skills that define the New Operating Class in the current era — context architecture, constraint design, iterative refinement, verification discipline — remain valuable in an ARI environment. But they are supplemented by something new: the capacity to engage with a reasoning partner rather than merely direct a generation engine. The operator who can identify when an ARI system's reasoning is genuinely sound versus when its apparent confidence masks a logical error will hold substantially more leverage than the operator who treats ARI outputs as authoritative because they are sophisticated.

Verification discipline, in other words, does not become less important when systems become more capable. It becomes more important — because the gap between 'sounds right' and 'is right' becomes harder to detect as the reasoning becomes more sophisticated.

10.11 The Acceleration and Its Implications

The AI-assists-AI loop means the transition from current AI to ARI may arrive faster than most projections suggest — not because any single breakthrough will produce it, but because the compounding improvement rate makes capability jumps that would have taken a decade happen in years.

This creates a specific planning challenge for individuals and organizations. Systems that are genuinely useful today may be superseded by systems with qualitatively different capabilities within a planning horizon that most professionals use for career and organizational strategy. The operator who designs their AI competency development for the systems available today may find those competencies partially obsolete by 2029 — not because the skills are wrong, but because the systems have moved.

The response to this is not anxiety about the pace of change. It is architectural thinking about which skills are durable across the transition and which are specific to current systems.

The durable skills are the ones closest to human judgment: the capacity to evaluate reasoning quality rather than output fluency, the discipline to verify rather than accept, the domain expertise that makes anomalies visible, and the accountability that no AI system can assume. These skills remain valuable regardless of whether the system being used is probabilistic synthesis or multi-agent reasoning. The underlying human value proposition — judgment, accountability, contextual wisdom — is not what the AI-assists-AI loop is compressing.

What it is compressing is everything that was previously called knowledge work but was actually pattern-following with professional credentials attached. The distinction matters enormously for how individuals invest in their own development and how organizations design their AI integration strategies.

Final Principle: Labor Redefined by Leverage — and Leverage About to Change

Synthetic labor is not ultimately about automation. It is about the restructuring of cognitive work — the compression of coordination, synthesis, analysis, drafting, and operational throughput in ways that change the relationship between human effort and organizational output.

But the full picture today requires holding two things simultaneously. First: the compression is real, substantial, and already reshaping professional leverage in every domain touched by knowledge work. Second: the compression is not the endpoint. The AI-assists-AI dynamic is producing capability improvements at a rate that makes today's powerful systems look, in retrospect, like early iterations.

ARI — multi-agent consensus reasoning with emergent common sense — is the next stage. Its arrival will not be announced by a single product launch or research paper. It will emerge gradually from the accumulation of incremental improvements, each individually explicable, collectively transformative.

The operators, organizations, and societies that navigate that transition most effectively will not be the ones who predicted its timing most precisely. They will be the ones who understood its nature — and built human capabilities robust enough to remain essential inside it.

CHAPTER 11

THE PSYCHOLOGY OF MACHINE PERSUASION

Behavioral Influence, Linguistic Control, and the ARI Horizon

Language does not merely transmit information. It shapes how information is received, interpreted, emotionally weighted, and acted upon. This has been understood by rhetoricians since Aristotle, by political strategists since Machiavelli, and by advertising researchers since the early twentieth century. Language, deployed skillfully, is not description — it is architecture. It builds the interpretive frameworks within which facts become meaningful, determines which comparisons feel natural, and activates the emotional states that make certain conclusions feel obvious and others feel uncomfortable.

AI systems dramatically amplify the capacity to deploy language strategically at scale. A skilled human writer might produce several thousand words of strategically framed content per day. An AI system can produce millions of words of strategically framed content per hour, adapted to specific audiences, optimized for specific emotional effects, and personalized to individual behavioral profiles. The rhetorical knowledge that previously required human expertise and human effort is now accessible to anyone who can construct the right prompts.

Natural CodeLex calls this emerging reality Machine Persuasion: the use of AI systems to generate language specifically designed to influence perception, activate emotional states, shape interpretive frames, and direct behavior — at scales and speeds that exceed what human communication alone can achieve.

Understanding machine persuasion is essential for any serious operator today. Not just because of its risks — though those are real and documented — but because persuasion is embedded in virtually every AI-assisted communication workflow, whether the operator recognizes it or not. Every framing choice is a persuasion choice. Every AI-generated document makes interpretive decisions that shape how the reader receives what follows. The operator who does not understand machine persuasion is making those choices unconsciously. The operator who understands it makes them deliberately.

11.1 Framing in Action: One Event, Five Realities

The persuasive power of language lies primarily not in what it says but in how it frames what it says — what it makes salient, what it backgrounds, what comparisons it implies, what emotional register it establishes. The following demonstrates this through a single scenario framed five different ways:

```
SCENARIO: A technology company announces it is
eliminating 18% of its workforce.

FRAMING 1 — CORPORATE ANNOUNCEMENT:
'We are making strategic adjustments to our
organizational structure to ensure we are best
positioned for the opportunities ahead. These
thoughtful changes will allow us to invest more
deeply in the areas where we see the greatest
potential, while treating all affected colleagues
with the respect and support they deserve during
this transition.'
PSYCHOLOGICAL ACTIVATION: Future-orientation.
Organizational agency. Employee dignity. No
mention of financial pressure or personal
disruption. Emotional register: calm, forward-
looking.

FRAMING 2 — LABOR ADVOCACY:
'The company has eliminated 18% of its workforce
— roughly 4,200 jobs — after posting record
profits last year. Workers who built the
company's success are being discarded while
executive compensation packages remain intact.
This is not a difficult business decision. It is
a values decision.'
PSYCHOLOGICAL ACTIVATION: Moral framing. Contrast
between worker sacrifice and executive
```

```
protection. Rejection of the neutralizing frame.
Emotional register: moral outrage.

FRAMING 3 — FINANCIAL ANALYST:
'The restructuring represents approximately $180M
in annualized savings and improves operating
margin by approximately 2.3 percentage points.
Execution risk is moderate given the
concentration of eliminated roles in product
development functions.'
PSYCHOLOGICAL ACTIVATION: Numerical authority.
Human impact disappears entirely — 18% of a
workforce becomes margin improvement. Emotional
register: analytical detachment.

FRAMING 4 — MEDIA REPORTING:
'The company announced Tuesday that it would cut
18% of its staff in the largest single reduction
in its history. The move came weeks after the
company reported its strongest quarter in three
years.'
PSYCHOLOGICAL ACTIVATION: The juxtaposition of
'strongest quarter' and 'largest reduction'
implies tension without stating it. Emotional
register: neutral framing that still constructs a
story.

FRAMING 5 — POLITICAL MESSAGING:
'While workers paid the price for the company's
pivot to automation, shareholders saw their
returns increase 34% over the same period. This
is the human cost of unchecked corporate power —
and it's happening in communities like yours.'
PSYCHOLOGICAL ACTIVATION: Causal attribution.
Fear and solidarity. Geographic personalization.
Emotional register: urgency, injustice.
```

Five framings of the identical event. Each activates entirely different emotional states, assigns different moral responsibility, and makes different actors salient or invisible. AI systems can generate all five with equal facility, adapt each to specific audience profiles, and deploy them at whatever scale the communicator requires.

11.2 The Behavioral Science Foundation

Machine persuasion derives its power from well-documented psychological mechanisms that make humans systematically susceptible to specific types of linguistic influence.

```
FRAMING EFFECTS (Kahneman & Tversky, 1979):
The same outcome described as gains versus losses
produces systematically different decisions even
when expected value is identical. '90% survival
rate' and '10% mortality rate' describe the same
outcome but produce different patient decisions.
AI can generate whichever framing serves the
objective — and A/B test framings at scale to
identify which produces the desired behavioral
response most reliably.

NARRATIVE TRANSPORTATION (Green & Brock, 2000):
When humans are engaged by a story, critical
evaluation of claims made within that story
decreases significantly. People inside a
narrative evaluate claims less analytically than
people in an analytical mode. AI systems generate
engaging narrative framing for any content with
remarkable facility — systematically invoking the
effect that reduces critical scrutiny.

SOCIAL PROOF AND NORMALIZATION:
Humans are strongly influenced by information
about what others do and believe. Framing
behavior as common, endorsed, or consistent with
group identity significantly increases compliance
rates. AI systems can generate social proof
framing at scale and personalize it to specific
audience profiles.

EMOTIONAL PRIMING:
Exposure to emotionally loaded content changes
subsequent information processing. Fear-primed
users evaluate information more risk-aversively.
Hope-primed users evaluate it more
optimistically. AI systems can construct
contextual emotional environments that prime
specific interpretive responses before delivering
the core message.

AUTHORITY SIGNALING:
Humans grant credibility to sources displaying
markers of expertise — specific vocabulary,
organized argument structure, professional tone.
AI systems reliably produce these authority
```

```
signals for any content — including content that
would not warrant them from a genuine expert.
```

11.3 The Ethical Spectrum

Machine persuasion exists on a spectrum from legitimate communication to deliberate manipulation — and the line between them is genuinely contested rather than clearly defined.

```
CLEARLY LEGITIMATE:
A nonprofit uses AI to generate donor
communications that better explain measurable
impact. The information is accurate. The
emotional activation is appropriate to the actual
context.

A public health agency uses AI to generate
vaccination communication addressing the specific
concerns of vaccine-hesitant communities, using
framing more likely to engage than default
clinical language. The goal is accurate
information, more accessibly presented.

ETHICALLY CONTESTED:
A pharmaceutical company uses AI to frame modest
efficacy data in language emphasizing positive
findings while technically disclosing limitations
in forms most readers will not process — fine
print, statistical language, buried
qualifications.

A financial services company generates investment
communications emphasizing favorable historical
returns while presenting risk disclosures in
formats designed to minimize their psychological
impact. Technically compliant. Designed to reduce
the behavioral impact of required disclosures.

CLEARLY MANIPULATIVE:
A political organization generates micro-targeted
messaging activating fear responses through
selective presentation of technically true but
deliberately distorted statistics.

An influence operation generates synthetic social
media personas simulating organic grassroots
```

```
support for positions serving a specific
interest.
```

The ethically contested cases are the most commonly encountered in real organizational AI deployment. The question 'when does optimization become manipulation?' does not have a clean algorithmic answer. It requires judgment about intent, effect, power differential, and whether the optimization is toward clarity or toward behavioral compliance regardless of genuine understanding.

11.4 Persuasion Literacy as Civic Infrastructure

As AI-generated communication becomes widespread, societies require new cognitive infrastructure for navigating it. Persuasion literacy is the capacity to evaluate not just what a communication says but how it has been constructed to produce a specific cognitive and emotional effect.

Traditional media literacy — focused on source evaluation and factual accuracy — is necessary but insufficient for the machine persuasion era. A communication can be entirely factually accurate and still be profoundly manipulative through selective framing. Factual accuracy evaluation does not catch framing manipulation.

Persuasion literacy requires different questions: What emotional state is this communication designed to activate, and is that activation appropriate to the information conveyed? What information is absent that would be relevant to a fully informed judgment? What action is this communication designed to produce, and does the evidence actually support it?

These questions are teachable. They are also increasingly necessary — not just for political participation and consumer decision-making, but for professional judgment in any domain where AI-generated content influences decisions. The professional who cannot evaluate machine-generated framing is increasingly the professional who cannot evaluate the analytical environment they are operating in.

11.5 A Real Failure: When Optimization Becomes Manipulation

The following pattern emerged from documented organizational communication analysis and is representative of a class of failures that emerge when AI-generated communication is optimized for organizational objectives rather than transparency.

A technology company facing significant restructuring used AI to generate internal communications for different employee populations. The stated goal was clarity and empathy. The actual workflow became something more troubling.

The communications team generated different versions of the same restructuring announcement for different employee groups, optimized for different emotional responses. The version sent to affected employees emphasized support structures — severance, outplacement, extended benefits. The version sent to retained employees emphasized strategic vision and growth trajectory.

Both communications were technically accurate. Neither contained false information. What they were not was honest. Affected employees received communications optimized to reduce likelihood of legal action. Retained employees received communications optimized to prevent attrition. The optimization targets were organizational risk mitigation, not genuine transparency.

When the differential communications leaked, the reputational damage was substantially worse than the restructuring itself would have generated. The revelation that different groups had received strategically different framings of the same event produced a collapse of organizational trust that persisted well beyond the restructuring.

The failure was not technological. The AI produced exactly what it was asked to produce. The failure was a category error about what optimization means in human communication contexts. The technology did not create the ethical question. It scaled it.

11.6 Adaptive Persuasion at Scale

Traditional media is relatively static. A speech, advertisement, or article is generally fixed once published. The same message reaches all audiences in the same form.

AI systems can adapt messaging dynamically — generating personalized persuasive content for specific audiences, optimizing framing based on behavioral feedback, and scaling individually tailored communication to previously impossible volumes. A political campaign can now generate individually adapted policy messaging for thousands of demographic micro-segments simultaneously. A company can produce customer communications personalized to emotional profiles derived from behavioral data.

The persuasion asymmetry this creates is historically significant. A single operator with a well-constructed AI workflow can produce persuasive content at a scale previously requiring entire media organizations. The individual or organization that understands machine persuasion deeply enough to deploy it deliberately has leverage that no prior communications technology provided.

This asymmetry is not inherently dangerous. Legitimate organizations communicating accurately and effectively with large audiences is a genuine social good. The danger lies in the combination of scale, personalization, and reduced friction for deploying manipulative framing — because the same capabilities that serve legitimate communication serve manipulation with equal efficiency.

11.7 Machine Persuasion in the ARI Era

Everything in this chapter describes machine persuasion as it exists today — AI systems capable of generating strategically framed language at scale, adapting to audience profiles, and producing authority signals for any position on any topic.

The ARI era will intensify these dynamics significantly.

Current AI generates plausible persuasive language. It produces framings that are statistically associated with persuasive communication patterns in its training data. The framing is often effective because the patterns it draws on are genuinely associated with persuasive outcomes. But it is not reasoning about what would persuade a specific person given their specific cognitive profile, their specific prior beliefs, and the specific conversational context.

ARI systems — capable of genuine multi-step reasoning rather than pattern completion — would be able to do exactly this. An ARI persuasion system would not generate statistically plausible persuasive language. It would reason about the target's belief structure, identify the specific logical and emotional levers most likely to shift their position, construct a communication sequence that leads them through that shift, and adapt in real time based on their responses.

This is not a hypothetical future capability. It is the logical extension of current trends into the next capability stage. The behavioral science foundations of persuasion are well-documented and increasingly machine-legible. The capacity to reason about individual cognitive profiles from behavioral data already exists in primitive form. ARI reasoning applied to persuasion would integrate these capabilities into a system whose sophistication exceeds anything currently deployed.

The governance challenge this creates is profound. Current regulatory frameworks for advertising, political messaging, and media influence were designed for human-scale communication — where the resources required to reach individuals with personalized persuasive messaging were substantial enough to limit its use to well-resourced actors with significant institutional accountability. ARI persuasion systems would eliminate the resource constraint while preserving the accountability gap.

11.8 The Consent Question

At the center of the machine persuasion challenge is a question about consent that existing frameworks have not adequately addressed.

When a human communicator frames a message strategically — choosing which facts to emphasize, which emotional register to adopt, which comparisons to invoke — we generally accept this as the normal exercise of communicative skill. We expect communicators to frame messages in ways that serve their objectives. We hold them accountable when those framings cross into deception.

Machine persuasion does not change this basic dynamic. But it changes the scale, the precision, and the detectability. At human scale, strategic framing is a skill that requires effort, limits the number of distinct messages that can be crafted, and is generally visible in the choices made. At machine scale, strategic framing is automated, unlimited in volume, precisely personalized, and often invisible in the sense that readers cannot readily identify what choices were made and why.

The question of consent in this environment is: did the recipient of a machine-persuasion communication consent to receive a communication specifically optimized to shift their beliefs or behaviors? In most current deployments, the answer is no — not because anyone asked them and they refused, but because the question was never raised. The communication was received as a normal communication, not as a persuasion-optimized output of an AI system analyzing their behavioral profile.

Whether this matters morally depends on whether you believe that the absence of overt deception makes strategic framing ethically neutral. The evidence from the failure case in this chapter suggests that people feel differently about this when they discover it after the fact — which is itself informative about the implicit consent expectations people bring to communication.

11.9 Governance and the Detection Problem

Societies have historically regulated advertising, political messaging, and media influence through institutions designed for human-scale communication. AI systems alter that scale entirely — and regulatory frameworks are struggling to adapt.

The detection problem is central. Traditional fraud and manipulation law depends on being able to demonstrate that a specific communication was false or that specific misleading claims were made. Machine persuasion that operates entirely through framing — selecting true facts, organizing them strategically, activating specific emotional states through legitimate rhetorical choices — does not produce the kind of demonstrably false claims that existing fraud frameworks can address.

Emerging governance responses include synthetic content disclosure requirements, AI-generated media labeling, behavioral advertising restrictions, and platform transparency obligations. These represent early-stage institutional responses to a challenge whose full scope is not yet visible. They are also largely reactive — responding to capabilities that have already been deployed widely enough to produce documented harms.

The more fundamental governance challenge is not identifying specific bad actors using machine persuasion maliciously. It is designing systems that preserve meaningful consent in a communication environment where persuasion optimization is a default feature of AI-assisted communication, not an exceptional deployment.

Final Principle: Influence Requires Responsibility

Machine persuasion is not fundamentally about deception. It is about scalable influence — the capacity to deploy strategically framed language at scales and speeds that were previously impossible, with personalization precision that was previously unavailable.

The operators who understand this deeply are not necessarily the operators who will misuse it. Many of the most important applications of machine persuasion are genuinely beneficial — public health communication that reaches vaccine-hesitant populations more effectively, educational content that adapts to individual learning styles, organizational communication that actually gets read and understood rather than ignored.

The difference between beneficial deployment and harmful deployment is not technical. It is intentional. It is the difference between optimizing toward clarity and genuine understanding, and optimizing toward behavioral compliance regardless of whether the recipient's understanding supports the behavior being sought.

That distinction requires human judgment to maintain. AI systems will optimize toward whatever objective the operator specifies. They do not independently evaluate whether the objective is compatible with the recipient's genuine interests. That evaluation is the operator's responsibility — and it becomes more consequential, not less, as the persuasion capabilities of AI systems advance toward ARI.

The future of machine persuasion will not be shaped primarily by technology. It will be shaped by the choices operators make about what they optimize for — and by the governance frameworks that societies build to make those choices accountable.

CHAPTER 12

THE NEW OPERATING CLASS AND THE SOVEREIGNTY QUESTION

Who Gains Leverage — and What That Means for Human Civilization

Every major technological transition in the modern era has produced a class of operators — a group of people who learned the new system well enough, early enough, to gain leverage asymmetries over those who did not. The pattern is consistent and the mechanism is straightforward: when a powerful new technology creates new capabilities, the people who understand those capabilities deeply enough to deploy them strategically gain advantages that compound, because early leverage creates the resources and reputation that enable further advantage.

The industrial era produced factory owners, industrial engineers, and scientific managers who understood mechanical production and organizational efficiency when most workers were still adapting to factory rhythms. The internet era produced software builders, network architects, and platform designers who understood distributed systems when most businesses were still treating the web as a marketing channel. In each case, the early operators did not simply use the technology — they understood it at a level that allowed them to design with it, build systems from it, and recognize opportunities that later adopters would only see in retrospect.

The AI era is producing a similar transition. Natural CodeLex™ calls the emerging group the New Operating Class: individuals who understand cognitive systems, workflow orchestration, information architecture, synthetic reasoning, and AI leverage at a level that creates significant, compounding productivity advantage — and who combine that technical fluency with the human judgment, domain expertise, and ethical clarity that determines whether that leverage is directed productively.

12.1 The Historical Pattern

```
THE SCIENTIFIC MANAGEMENT ERA (1880s-1930s):
Frederick Winslow Taylor's systematic management
principles created the first professional class
explicitly defined by understanding how to
optimize production systems. Those who mastered
Taylorist principles gained leverage over
traditional craft-based managers. The transition
created new managerial roles and dramatically
improved industrial productivity, while
simultaneously deskilling craft workers and
concentrating organizational power in those who
controlled system design.

THE SOFTWARE ERA (1980s-2000s):
The personal computer and internet transitions
created operators who understood software
systems, network architecture, and data
infrastructure. Those who gained this fluency
early — programmers, systems administrators,
database architects — created and captured value
at scales that seemed implausible to those
operating with earlier mental models.

THE PLATFORM ERA (2000s-2010s):
Social media and platform economy transitions
created operators who understood attention
dynamics, network effects, and platform
architecture. The leverage gap between those who
understood these systems and those who did not
was enormous and sustained.

THE AI ERA (2020s-):
The current transition is producing operators who
understand cognitive system architecture,
probabilistic output generation, workflow
orchestration, and synthetic leverage. The
defining characteristic — compared to
predecessors — is breadth. Software operators had
leverage primarily in technology-adjacent
contexts. AI operators have leverage across
virtually every domain of cognitive work.
```

12.2 What Defines the New Operating Class

The New Operating Class is not defined by access to AI tools — those are becoming universally available. It is defined by the depth of understanding that produces the leverage differential: the combination of specific competencies that allow AI systems to be used not just as productivity tools but as genuine cognitive infrastructure.

```
COMPETENCY 1 — SYSTEMS THINKING:
The ability to understand AI outputs as products
of probabilistic systems with specific
properties, failure modes, and behavioral
tendencies. Systems thinkers ask not just 'Is
this output good?' but 'Why did the system
produce this, and under what conditions would it
produce something different?'

COMPETENCY 2 — VERIFICATION DISCIPLINE:
The consistent practice of evaluating AI outputs
with skepticism calibrated to stakes — checking
factual claims, identifying unsupported
inferences, recognizing hallucination patterns,
and maintaining critical evaluation even when
outputs seem authoritative.

COMPETENCY 3 — WORKFLOW ARCHITECTURE:
The ability to design AI workflows that match the
structure of complex problems — using iterative
refinement, phased analysis, adversarial review,
session segmentation, and contextual isolation
appropriately rather than applying generic
prompting uniformly.

COMPETENCY 4 — CONTEXTUAL MANAGEMENT:
The understanding of how context affects AI
behavior — building and maintaining effective
Context Stacks, recognizing and correcting
context drift and contamination, resetting when
necessary, and segmenting workflows by domain.

COMPETENCY 5 — RECURSIVE REASONING:
The ability to use recursive AI analysis
effectively — knowing when comparative reasoning,
adversarial critique, and multi-perspective
simulation improve decision quality and when they
produce diminishing returns.
```

12.3 Stratification Risks and Access Gaps

The emergence of a New Operating Class is not an unambiguously positive development. It carries stratification risks that deserve honest acknowledgment — not as arguments against AI adoption, but as arguments for deliberate policy and institutional responses.

Educational access gaps mean students at well-resourced institutions in high-income economies are developing AI workflow skills years ahead of students in under-resourced environments. The leverage gap this creates may compound across careers in ways that reproduce and amplify existing inequality patterns. Workers whose economic value was primarily derived from the procedural cognitive labor that AI compression most effectively replaces face genuine displacement risk that is not hypothetical or distant — it is occurring now.

Organizational concentration is another concern. AI leverage may amplify the advantages of organizations that can invest in sophisticated AI infrastructure over those that cannot, creating concentration dynamics that reverse some of the democratizing effects of the internet era. And cognitive stratification — the divide between those who develop strong AI fluency and those who do not — may not be primarily a function of intelligence or formal education. It may be a function of deliberate practice and early access, creating a form of stratification less correlated with existing credentialing systems than previous economic divides.

Acknowledging these risks is the necessary precondition for designing responses to them. Educational systems that teach AI fluency broadly, workforce transition programs that support displaced workers, regulatory frameworks that prevent AI leverage from producing monopolistic concentration, and organizational cultures that invest in broad-based AI skill development are all legitimate responses. None becomes visible as a priority if the stratification risks are dismissed as secondary to the productivity gains.

12.4 Strategic Sovereignty: The Defining Characteristic

Among the characteristics that define the most effective members of the New Operating Class, strategic sovereignty — the use of AI systems as leverage tools while maintaining independent human judgment — stands out as the most important and the most difficult to sustain.

Strategic sovereignty is not technological skepticism. Operators who maintain it use AI extensively and productively. They are not the people who avoid AI to preserve their analytical independence. They are the people who use AI aggressively while maintaining the cognitive discipline to evaluate what it produces rather than simply acting on it. They resist the authority pressure that makes confident-sounding outputs feel reliable. They resist the efficiency pressure that makes verification feel like an unnecessary cost. They resist the atrophy pressure that makes it easy to stop practicing the analytical skills that AI convenience is making less necessary.

The New Operating Class is not simply the people who use AI most intensively. It is the people who use AI most intelligently — understanding where it creates genuine leverage, where it introduces risk, and where human judgment must remain primary.

12.5 The Sovereignty Question

The New Operating Class is emerging. The leverage asymmetries are real. The productivity gains are substantial. And all of this raises a question that cannot be answered by any individual operator optimizing their own workflows — a question that belongs to civilization rather than to any single person or organization.

If a class of operators is gaining asymmetric leverage through AI systems, and if those AI systems are simultaneously mediating how billions of people access information, form judgments, communicate, and make decisions — what does it mean to remain a genuinely sovereign cognitive agent in that environment? What does it mean for a society to maintain genuine democratic self-governance when the information environment is increasingly shaped by synthetic systems? What does it mean for human institutions to maintain legitimate authority when AI can replicate many of their analytical functions?

Natural CodeLex calls this the Sovereignty Question. It is not a question about whether AI becomes conscious or whether machines surpass human intelligence in some general sense. It is a much more immediate and practical question about what it means to preserve genuine human agency — cognitive, informational, political, and institutional — as synthetic cognition becomes progressively more capable, more integrated, and more infrastructural.

12.6 Four Dimensions of Human Sovereignty Under Pressure

```
COGNITIVE SOVEREIGNTY:
The capacity to reason through complex problems
independently – to analyze, synthesize, and reach
conclusions without delegating the cognitive
process to synthetic systems. It is threatened
not by any single act of outsourcing but by the
gradual pattern of outsourcing that makes
independent reasoning increasingly unfamiliar and
eventually uncomfortable.

INFORMATIONAL SOVEREIGNTY:
The capacity to access, evaluate, and interpret
information independently – to engage with
primary sources, evaluate competing claims, and
form judgments without depending on a single
synthesis intermediary. When the same system
synthesizes information for hundreds of millions
of people simultaneously, the interpretive
choices embedded in that synthesis gain outsized
influence over collective understanding.

POLITICAL SOVEREIGNTY:
The collective capacity of democratic societies
to form genuine public opinion through authentic
deliberation – opinion formation that reflects
actual citizen values rather than AI-amplified
influence campaigns. Machine persuasion
```

```
capabilities allow influence actors to generate
personalized political messaging at scales and
precision previously impossible.

INSTITUTIONAL SOVEREIGNTY:
The capacity of human institutions – governments,
courts, universities, professional bodies – to
maintain legitimate authority in domains where AI
systems can replicate many of their traditional
functions. The institutions that provide
professional expertise exist partly because they
create accountability. AI systems that replicate
the functions without the accountability create
legitimacy vacuums that existing governance
frameworks are not equipped to fill.
```

12.7 A Civilizational Transition: Four Precedents

Every major technological transition transformed more than it appeared to transform from the inside. The printing press looked, to contemporaries, like a more efficient way to copy books. It turned out to be a reorganization of religious authority, political power, and scientific knowledge that unfolded over two centuries. Industrialization looked like a change in production methods. It turned out to be a reorganization of family structure, urban geography, and class identity whose consequences we are still navigating.

Electrification seemed straightforwardly beneficial in retrospect but was experienced as deeply disruptive — displacing craft industries, restructuring labor markets, creating new vulnerabilities. The internet democratized information access and communication, created new economic forms, and fundamentally changed how social relationships are organized — while also creating new vectors for misinformation, new mechanisms of addiction and attention capture, and new concentrations of economic and informational power.

Each of these transitions shares a common feature: it was significantly more transformative than it appeared from the inside, it produced both extraordinary benefits and genuine disruptions, and the institutional adaptations required to manage its implications took much longer to develop than the technological capabilities themselves. AI gives no reason to expect a different pattern — and the AI transition is occurring at significantly higher speed than its predecessors.

12.8 The Delegation Problem and Cognitive Atrophy

The deepest long-term risk of the AI transition is not sudden displacement. It is gradual delegation — the slow outsourcing of cognitive capacities that, going unpracticed, atrophy.

Research on GPS navigation provides an instructive parallel. People who rely primarily on GPS develop weaker allocentric spatial representations — the mental maps that allow navigation without external guidance — than people who navigate using landmarks and internal maps. The capability that goes unpracticed weakens. The important question is not whether GPS weakens spatial reasoning — it likely does, to some degree. The important question is whether the weakened capacity matters for purposes beyond navigation itself. The answer appears to be yes.

For AI and analytical reasoning, the stakes are higher. Analytical reasoning — the capacity to engage critically with evidence, evaluate competing explanations, identify unsupported inferences, and reach calibrated conclusions — is not merely useful for specific tasks. It is foundational to informed citizenship, professional judgment, and adaptive thinking in genuinely novel situations. If the convenience of AI synthesis gradually reduces the practice of doing analytical synthesis yourself, the cognitive capacity for independent analytical judgment may weaken in populations that no longer practice it regularly.

12.9 Strategic Responsibility: The Only Viable Path

Two inadequate responses frame the available options, and both should be rejected.

Techno-utopianism holds that AI represents unambiguous progress, that the risks are manageable, and that the appropriate posture is enthusiastic adoption. This underestimates the structural challenges that cognitive infrastructure transitions create. The historical precedents all produced genuine and serious disruptions alongside their genuine benefits. Optimism about AI's potential is warranted. Optimism that bypasses serious engagement with its risks is not.

Techno-pessimism holds that AI represents a fundamental threat and that the appropriate posture is resistance. This underestimates both the genuine benefits of AI systems and the human capacity for institutional adaptation. Societies have navigated profound technological transitions before. There is no principled reason to believe the AI transition is uniquely unsurvivable.

Strategic responsibility is the viable path between them — engaging with AI systems fully while maintaining deliberate discipline around the dimensions of human sovereignty that require active preservation.

> USING AI TO AMPLIFY HUMAN JUDGMENT rather than replace it – designing workflows that combine AI synthesis efficiency with human domain knowledge, verification discipline, and accountability.
>
> MAINTAINING ANALYTICAL PRACTICES that AI convenience creates pressure to abandon – not as an end in itself, but because those practices produce cognitive capacities that serve purposes beyond any specific task.
>
> BUILDING INSTITUTIONAL FRAMEWORKS that preserve transparency, contestability, and accountability in AI-mediated systems – so that the interpretive choices embedded in synthesis infrastructure are visible and challengeable.
>
> DEVELOPING PERSUASION LITERACY broadly – so that populations can evaluate AI-generated communication critically rather than accepting its framing defaults.
>
> INVESTING IN BROAD-BASED AI FLUENCY – so that the leverage advantages of the New Operating Class

> are accessible to broad populations rather than concentrated in the already-advantaged.
>
> PRESERVING THE INSTITUTIONS that create accountability – professional licensing, judicial review, democratic deliberation – even as AI systems replicate some of their analytical functions, because the accountability itself cannot be synthesized.

Final Principle: Sovereignty as Active Practice

The New Operating Class is emerging from the convergence of AI systems, cognitive infrastructure understanding, workflow architecture skill, and the judgment to deploy these capabilities with strategic sovereignty. The future advantage increasingly belongs not to the people with the most information, but to the people who understand how to architect systems, manage synthetic cognition, preserve judgment, and operate effectively inside AI-mediated environments.

And yet the emergence of that class, and the extraordinary leverage it commands, makes the Sovereignty Question not less urgent but more so. The more powerful the operating class, the more important it becomes that the civilization within which it operates preserves the cognitive independence, informational diversity, and institutional accountability that keep power answerable.

Sovereignty is not maintained passively. It requires the deliberate exercise of independent reasoning — not as resistance to AI, but as the discipline that makes AI genuinely useful rather than merely convenient. It requires verification habits that prevent synthetic authority from substituting for genuine analytical quality. It requires educational investment in the capabilities that AI cannot replicate. It requires the institutional frameworks that preserve accountability when AI systems are deployed in consequential domains.

The Art of Instruction — which is what this book has ultimately been about — is not just the skill of directing AI systems effectively. It is the deeper discipline of remaining genuinely in charge of what those systems produce, what they influence, and what they shape in the world.

Natural CodeLex began with a practical observation: that prompting is not about talking to machines but about designing cognitive environments. It ends with a larger one: that as those environments scale from individual workflows to civilizational infrastructure, the design choices we make — about what to automate and what to preserve, what to accelerate and what to govern, what to trust and what to question — will shape the cognitive future of human civilization.

The architecture of AI interaction is, ultimately, the architecture of the mind we are building for the future. And sovereignty — individual, institutional, and civilizational — is the decision to ensure that mind remains genuinely our own.

www.ingramcontent.com/pod-product-compliance
Lightning Source LLC
LaVergne TN
LVHW022220200926
848481LV00006B/2052

9798950938009